*The Forty-Three Guiding Principles
for an Enlightened Mind*

བྱང་ཆུབ་སེམས་ཀྱི་བསླབ་པ་བཞི་བཅུ་ཞེ་གསུམ་པ་
བཞུགས་སོ།།

Forty-Three Guiding Principles
for an
Enlightened Mind

Verses Composed by His Holiness,
the 21ˢᵗ sMenri Trizin, Kündun Sonam Lodrö

Translation and Commentary by
Latri Khenpo Nyima Dakpa Rinpoche

Dream Abbey
4 Covewood Court
Arden, NC 28704 USA
dreamabbey.com

© 2025 Latri Nyima Dakpa Rinpoche. All rights reserved.

No part of this book may be reproduced or translated in any form or by any means, electronic or mechanical, including photography, recording, or by any information storage and retrieval system or technologies now known or later developed, without permission in writing from the publisher.

Printed on acid-free paper.

Library of Congress Control Number: 2025930075

ISBN 978-1-951105-10-5 (paperback)
ISBN 978-1-951105-11-2 (ebook)

Contents

Preface xi

Introduction 1

Verse of Praise 7
    1. Verse of Praise 8

Commitment 15
    2. Commitment 16

Preliminaries 21
    3. Making a Meaningful Life 22
    4. Eliminating the Source of the Three Poisons 28
    5. Hermitage, the Source of Inner Qualities 35
    6. Following the Lama, the Source of Blessings 39
    7. Entering the Path of Virtue 45
    8. Practice on Impermanence 49
    9. Going to Refuge in the Four Supreme Objects 53

Actual Practice 59
   10. Avoiding Non-virtuous Deeds 60
   11. Searching the Path of Freedom 68
   12. Generating the Mind of Enlightenment 72
   13. Exchanging Your Happiness with One Who is
       Suffering 82
   14. Bringing Robbery onto the Path 89
   15. Bringing Annihilation onto the Path 92
   16. Taking Gossip as the Path 95
   17. Taking Criticism as the Path 97
   18. Apply Practice to Mistreatment by One's Own Family
       100
   19. How to Treat Outsiders Who Mistreat You 102
   20. How to Apply Poverty and Downfall in the Path ... 104
   21. Understanding How to Be Satisfied 106
   22. How to Subdue Inner Wildness 109
   23. How to Overcome Attachment 112
   24. Non-Dual Contemplation 115
   25. Understanding the Truthlessness of Pleasantness ... 120
   26. Understanding the Truthlessness of Unpleasantness
       123
   27. Understanding the Truthlessness of Suffering 126
   28. Practice of Generosity 129
   29. Practice of Morality 133
   30. Practice of Patience 135
   31. Practice of Diligence 137
   32. Practice of Concentration 139
   33. Practice of Wisdom 142

34. Searching Your Own Delusions 144
35. Avoiding Meaningless Talk 146
36. Detaching from Materialism 148
37. Avoiding Harsh Speech 150
38. Ways to Renounce Ignorance 151
39. Advice for Serving Others 153
40. Dedication of Practice 154

Conclusion 157
41. Genuine Practice 158
42. Acknowledgement 160
43. Dedication and Aspirational Prayer 161

བྱང་ཆུབ་སེམས་ཀྱི་བསླབ་པ་བཞི་བཅུ་ཞེ་གསུམ་པ་འདི་ཉིད་དབྱིན་སྐད་དུ་བསྒྱུར་ནས་
པར་དུ་བསྐྲུན་པའི་དགེ་བ་འདུན་ནི། སྐྱབས་མཆོག་རྩ་བའི་བླ་མ་རྒྱལ་བ་སྨན་རིའི་
ཡོངས་འཛིན་སྐུ་བའི་མེད་གི་མཆོག་བསྟན་དང་འགྲོ་བའི་དཔལ་དུ་ཞབས་པད་དགུང་
གྲངས་བརྒྱ་ཡི་བར་དུ་བརྟན་ཅིང་བཞུགས་པའི་ཐུགས་རྗེ་ལེགས་གསོལ་མཆོད་བྱེད་
དང་། སྲིད་གསུང་རིན་པོ་ཆེ་མཆོག་ཉིད་འཆི་མེད་ཚེ་དབང་རིག་འཛིན་གྱི་རྡོ་རྗེ་གཡོ་
མེད་བཞུགས་པར་གསོལ་བ་འདེབས་པའི་སྙེན་དུ། རྗེ་ཉིད་ཀྱི་ཞལ་སློབ་ཡོངས་ཀྱི་གྲལ་
མཐའ་བ་བླ་ཁྲི་ཉི་མ་གྲགས་པས་༢༠༢༤/༡༡/༡༨་ཉིན།

The English translation and publishing of these Forty-Three Guiding Principles of Enlightened Mind is dedicated as an expression of deep gratitude to His Eminence, the supreme refuge, my root lama, sMenri's glorious principal tutor, Yongdzin Mawé Senge, who for one hundred years has preserved the teachings for the sake of all sentient beings.

Additionally, a prayer to request that Rinpoche remain steadfastly in the form of the immortal Lord of Longevity, Tsewang Rigdzin.

A humble disciple of His Eminence,
Latri Nyima Dakpa.
2024/11/18.

Preface

This text, the Forty-Three Guiding Principles for an Enlightened Mind, was written by His Holiness, Kündun Sonam Lodrö (also known as Kündun Sherab Gongyal), who was born in 1784 and passed away in 1835. Originally from Gyalrong, he was the 21st sMenri Trizin—the 21st throne holder of sMenri Monastery in Tibet.

While many other texts and teachings are transmitted by various deities, Khadro, and Enlightened Ones, His Holiness composed this text himself by thinking very carefully, "What is most needed in our everyday life?"

This text is not only for religious people. Everyone, as human beings living on this earth, experiences both happiness and sorrow—the ups and downs of this life. Based on those experiences, he wrote these forty-three stanzas. Each of the stanzas are well thought-out and organized. They discuss the real experiences and challenges we are all facing every day. For example, today everything may be good, but tomorrow there may be an obstacle. Today you may have everything, and tomorrow you may have nothing. But how do we deal with this? When we have everything, how do we make our day meaningful? And similarly, when we have nothing, how do we make our day meaningful?

Days are differentiated by our momentary experiences. And whether our momentary experience is productive or nonproductive is based on how well we are acknowledging its momentary nature and implementing our thoughtful quality of mind.

This text is not only about believing in protectors, Yidams, and Lamas. It's about how wide, flexible, and knowledgeable our conventional mind is. It's about how we act in any situation. For example, what do we do when our family members, loved ones, or trusted ones disrespect and abuse us? Or when people fool us—people who we would never expect such actions from? When these situations inevitably happen, how are we going to handle them to avoid any wrongdoing or causing additional unhappiness and sorrow? How can we look at the situation from another angle and use the experience to develop a more productive way of thinking and acting?

Each of these stanzas provides rich wisdom and knowledge. At the same time, they are very practical. While not all of these stanzas present a high meditation technique, each is still important and powerful. Each stanza makes a huge difference in our life if we mindfully read it, contemplate it, watch our minds, and apply the stanza's meaning in practice.

PREFACE

I have been teaching from this text for several years to many students in different places. I have applied the teachings myself. I have experienced, realized, and confirmed that this teaching is like a life-tonic for making life very productive. Having taught this, and having received a good response from my students, I decided to make the teaching into a book.

This book is not just for believers or religious people. It is truly for anyone who is open, with a mind that is like an empty paper on which you can draw anything. If your mind is flexible in this way, you can use these practices even if you don't have a religious outlook. With a feeling of joy and happiness, you can witness and develop your mind. You can gain positive experience.

If you study these stanzas, if you try to understand their meaning, and if you diligently apply the practice in real life, you will see the difference they make—from negative to positive, bad to good, sadness to happiness. Already, many people have been using it, applying it, and finding the results positive and helpful.

I have explained each stanza with my commentary. Read the stanza, work to understand it, then sit and meditate.

Throughout your life, as you go through experiences, mindfully recall whichever stanza matches your experience. If someone is insulting you in public, remember the stanza that talks about this, think about the meaning as I have detailed in the commentary, and apply the practice in that moment. This is how we can make our mind clean, clear, peaceful, and happy—by knowing how to let go, how to forgive, how to generate positive thought, and so on.

I believe and trust that this effort will bear a fruit and be of benefit to readers, whether they are my students, practitioners, or anyone else.

I have planned my books to take readers through the stages of Bön practice. This book is the beginning. It opens the practitioner to a spiritual life and an understanding of enlightened mind.

Then slowly, with good understanding, readers can choose to go deeper. While there are many books from many masters, with my books, you could next move on to *Opening the Door to Bön* to learn about the Ngöndro teachings and practices.

Following that, if you understand it, you may choose to move on to *The Inner Mirror*, which is about Dzogchen (Great Perfection), as well as onto *Khyung Mar* (Red Garuda), which is about healing in the Ngag (Skt. Tantra) tradition.

Following this path through my books will make a systematic development of your mind and practice.

Here, I would also like to thank those people who have been very helpful and supportive in many ways—transcribing, editing, and making this book beautiful. I would especially like to thank Nick Tichawa, my longtime student, who has been generous with his time, knowledge, and effort to complete everything beautifully. And I would also like to thank David Peteler, Deborah Peteler, Sarah Tichawa, and everyone who spent time editing and contributing to make this book beautiful.

It is my wish that this book be helpful and contribute to everyone's joy and happiness.

PREFACE

With my prayer and with my blessings, I wish you all a happy new year, 2025. I hope for everyone to be happy, healthy, joyful, and have a meaningful life.

Nyima Dakpa Rinpoche

Introduction

སྨྲ་བའི་སྨྲ་མཆོག་ཤེས་རབ་སྨྲ་སེང་ལ།
To the Lion of Speech, the Great Supreme Wisdom Deity,

རྣམ་པ་ཀུན་ཏུ་བཀའ་དྲིན་དྲན་པས་མཆོད།
We make offerings to you and always remember your kindness.

བྱང་ཆུབ་སེམས་ཀྱི་བསླབ་བྱ་བཤད་པ་ལ། མཆོད་བརྗོད་དམ་བཅའ་སྦྱོན་འགྲོ་དངོས་གཞི་མཇུག་དོན་ལྔ།
Concerning the exposition on the training of the mind of enlightenment [in] five [parts]: the Verse of Praise, Commitment, Preliminaries, Actual Practice, and Conclusion.

This teaching is known as the Forty-Three Guiding Principles or Instructions for an Enlightened Mind. These stanzas show us how to become a more genuine person—more loving, compassionate, and kind. We all have the potential for these qualities. Just as all the Enlightened Ones have achieved such qualities by performing the practices, we are also meant to enter this path by applying the practice in our lives.

We can benefit ourselves and others by understanding our own self—who we are and what we are—and by finding the sources of our ignorance and suffering.

The practice, if we apply it, makes us a bit gentler, more genuine, and more compassionate. We must be motivated to use this practice to create more positivity and dedicate it for the benefit for all sentient beings. This is the motivation of the Enlightened Ones—the *Buddha* (Sanskrit) or *Sangye* (Tibetan). Their motives are always for others' benefit, with the qualities of respect, love, and compassion for others.

As Tibetans prepare for Losar, Tibetan New Year, everyone prepares their altars, puts up thangkas, and cleans the altars and temples. Monks don't have many belongings, but they try to keep everything clean to welcome positive energy, merit, quality, and happiness. In the villages, people clean and try to remove things from their homes—all the things they have been holding onto needlessly all year. This symbolizes putting the garbage out. Not the material garbage, but the garbage we carry inside ourselves. We don't always realize how disordered our insides may be. We need to make the effort to fix that.

The master, Sonam Lodrö, His Holiness the 21st sMenri Tenzin, the spiritual head of Bön, composed these forty-three stanzas that we can apply in practice based on the teachings of Tönpa Shenrab, and the great masters' commentaries and teachings.

The forty-three stanzas are divided into five parts: 1.) Verse of Praise; 2.) Commitment; 3.) Preliminaries; 4.) Actual Practice; and 5.) Conclusion.

The stanzas are based on His Holiness's own experience of practice. He understood how we human beings act in our lives—how we chase after the five poisons (attachment, anger, ignorance, pride, and jealousy) and carry them with us. He understood how we can integrate the qualities of loving compassion, self-realization, and the transcendental practices. He realized this need we sentient beings have, and he wrote each of these forty-three stanzas so that we can focus on them in a practical way.

Don't think of the Forty-Three Guiding Principles as a guide that exists outside of yourself. The guide is inside. Bring yourself into the experience as your own guide within to make these forty-three verses effective in your own life.

It is my job to explain these guidelines the best I can. Then, your own understanding and level of effort is in your hands. Be your guide. Be your master. You are the key person to make a difference in your own mind. Not the master, nor the Enlightened One. You must guide your way.

I wish everyone good luck with this endeavor.

A Note on the Mind of Enlightenment

Semkyed means to literally "generate mind" or to think about something.

We always think very self-centered thoughts. We think thoughts about self, me, mine, etc. But we also can think more broadly—not only for the sake of oneself, but for the sake of other fellow beings, or even more broadly, for all sentient beings.

In practice, we are generating thought that is compassionate, broad, and beneficial to as large a group as possible—not just ourselves and our loved ones.

Yungdrung Sempa (sometimes translated as "Warm-hearted One," "Eternal Mind Hero," or "Bodhisattva" in Sanskrit) is what a person may eventually achieve through Semkyed practice. In Semkyed, when we "generate mind," the type of mind it is referring to is *jang chup kyi sem*, or enlightened mind.

However, we cannot completely generate an enlightened state of mind, because we are not yet Sangye. But we follow in the steps of those who have already walked the path and have achieved the result that we call "Sangye" or enlightenment.

Those who have already entered this path and have this very mind—though are not yet fully enlightened—are the Yungdrung Sempa. In addition to the Sangye, we are also following in their steps.

There are two main types of Semkyed: Mugpa Semkyed and Jugpa Semkyed.

Mugpa Semkyed is generating a mind of wishing good will—a beautiful mind for the benefit of others, full of concern for their wellbeing, feeling compassion and loving kindness towards them. Mugpa Semkyed is like aspiration, where we wish all sentient beings to be free from suffering. We may even wish that we can serve as the cause for their freedom from suffering. But at least, this type of Semkyed is about wishing good for others.

Jugpa Semkyed means putting into action that initial mugpa—that aspiration. Ultimately, it's not good enough to only wish well and do nothing. So, when our wish is broad and our mind is well-matured, this strengthening causes us to have the capacity to move into action. The initial wish that we had to serve sentient beings becomes the actions that are performed for the benefit and welfare of others.

Within Jugpa Semkyed there are both relative Semkyed and absolute Semkyed.

With relative Semkyed, we may not have yet fully realized the true nature of our minds or the nature of all phenomena; but if we have a virtuous, positive, pure, doubtless, unemotional, and spiritual mind that we use to genuinely dedicate for the welfare of others, this is relative Jugpa Semkyed. For example, we may recite Semkyed prayers, or prayers to eliminate obstacles for others, or to heal pains, or to remove suffering. We also generate mental states of love, kindness, and compassion for others and meditate on this. This level of thought, while pure, is still the relative Semkyed. It still depends on causes and conditions, and it exists on the level of the conventional world.

With absolute Semkyed, we realize the true nature of all phenomena and of our own mind within the nature of emptiness.

This emptiness realization is then both bound with, and based on, our conventional compassion—thoughts and actions of good will. Together, there is a union of these two truths in Semkyed.

Often it is advised, even in the Sutras, that it is not good enough to only have realized emptiness without having compassion and loving kindness. Realization of emptiness alone will not get us anywhere. It's only one side of what is necessary. For it to have meaningful benefit for others, we must also have compassion, loving kindness, and good will toward other beings.

I

Verse of Praise

1. Verse of Praise

དང་པོ་ནི།།
First:

བསྟན་དང་བསྟན་འཛིན་རྒྱས་ཤིང་འཕེལ་བའི་ཕྱིར།
For the spreading of the teaching and elevating the teacher
   [who holds the lineages],

འགྲོ་བའི་དོན་ལ་རབ་ཏུ་བརྩོན་མཛད་པ།
[Who] strives enthusiastically for the sake of sentient beings,

བླ་མ་སངས་རྒྱས་རིག་འཛིན་སེམས་དཔའི་ཚོགས།
Lama (Teacher), Sangye (Enlightened Ones), Community of
   Rigdzin (Knowledge Holders), [and] [Yungdrung] Sempa
   (Warm-hearted Ones),

རྟག་ཏུ་སྒོ་གསུམ་གུས་པས་ཕྱག་འཚལ་བསྟོད།
I continually bow and pay homage through the Three Doors
   (Body, Speech, and Mind).

It is important, as we begin, to be motivated with pure and good thoughts—to learn something we can apply to benefit oneself and others. This pure intention is very important. It makes a difference in the effects and result of our practice. Begin with this pure intention.

This first stanza is the verse of praise given to the Enlightened Ones and the Yungdrung Sempa—those who have discovered or realized the true mind of enlightenment. We pay respect to them truly, from inside, showing them respect through body, speech, and mind by prostrating to them.

We also praise the teachings of the Sangye and the lineage holders or masters who carry the teaching. In the Bön tradition, the transmission lineage is very important. It allows practitioners to recognize where the teaching comes from. The masters of the lineage are the sources of the teaching. We are connected to this teaching through our Lama (Teacher) and their Lama and so on.

Rigdzin, mentioned in the text, is a master according to the *Ngag* (Skt. Tantra) tradition. The word literally means "Knowledge Holder." In Ngag, there are stages of realization and accomplishment, and Rigdzins are those that have achieved a certain stage on the path according to Ngag. Rigdzins have discovered or achieved the realization of emptiness—the true nature of all phenomena—and have built up their compassion.

Similarly, the Sempa are the Warm-hearted Ones, those that have realized the warm-hearted compassion for all sentient beings. These beings, too, have great realization of emptiness.

Yungdrung Bön generally means, "Eternal Bön," but Yungdrung has other meanings, one of which is the union of relative and ultimate truths. The relative aspect is compassion, and the ultimate aspect is the true nature of all phenomena.

This means that our wisdom-realization of the true nature of our mind, like that of the Sangye, Rigdzin, Sempa, should be based on warm-hearted compassion. While we are meditating on emptiness or realizing emptiness, we shouldn't be separate from the realization of compassion. If we can practice these together inseparably—emptiness based on compassion—this is called an inseparable union of the methods or ways of skillful means and wisdom (Tib. *thab* and *sherab zung du drel wa*).

Compassion alone will not put us into the ultimate state of result of our practice. Similarly, only realizing the nature of existing phenomena will not bear the ultimate result. If we are only focusing on emptiness without a basis in compassion, then we are only experiencing wisdom without method. If we are focusing only on compassion, this is all well and good, but it does not ultimately liberate us from cyclic existence or ignorance, because there is no wisdom, and we will not reach the final attainment of enlightenment. To achieve enlightenment, we must have the inseparable union of emptiness and compassion.

So, what does this stanza teach us? What does it mean to make a prostration to Lamas, the Sangye, the Yungdrung Sempa, and the Bön scriptures in front of an altar or shrine? A prostration, bowing down and touching our legs, arms, and head to the floor, is a physical act showing our inner humility. Humility, in turn, can teach us in our day-to-day life how to respect our fellow beings.

Sometimes, we may experience a kind of wildness in ourselves, but truly, nobody is always wild inside. We also all have a potential of humility. We can all be simple and gentle. What this stanza teaches is more than the physical, external way of showing respect through the gesture of prostrating but how to apply it internally. The action of showing respect will make us gentler, more peaceful, humble, and simple—good human beings.

VERSE OF PRAISE

We need to learn how to bow down and pay respect to others. It doesn't mean only respecting those who have a politically, spiritually, monetarily, or materially high position. This may not be true respect; it is conditional. It is a respect that expects something in return. Instead, we are talking about showing respect because we truly value the person from within.

In this first stanza, the author is making a prostration to the teaching and all the lineage holders of the teachings. The source of happiness for self and others depends on the enlightened teachings. Therefore, the Enlightened Ones and highly realized ones are prostrated to. But in truth, every one of us has this potential, so we need to learn how to respect everyone in this way. This will make us simple and humble.

If we return to look at the stanza plainly, it is a simple showing of respect, offering prostrations, and appreciating the masters' accomplishment. We appreciate the Enlightened One who taught the masters, who in turn have kept or preserved this tradition. But, if we go deeper into this stanza, it's talking about appreciating the true sources of happiness, for which all sentient beings are searching.

The source of the happiness we are looking for is connected directly to the teachings of Sangye Tönpa Shenrab. To be of benefit, the teachings must be connected through the realized masters and Yungdrung Sempa who preserve the message and spread the great wisdom and compassion-essence of Bön.

The teaching or text itself is not able to talk directly to us. But to understand the teaching and implement it in our practice and everyday life, we are introduced through our teacher, who in turn learned through their masters. It is with their compassion, generosity, and wisdom that we understand the teachings with more clarity and detail. Then, with their support and encouragement, we apply these teachings, and we face the struggles in our path of practice.

The focus of this stanza should be about how much we understand—how much we connect with and acknowledge—that the source of true happiness is the teachings.

What makes you believe the teaching is the source of one's own and others' happiness?

This is something we must think about and discover for ourselves. When we look inside and get a satisfying answer for why the teaching is the source of our happiness, then we naturally have great respect toward the teaching and teacher who introduced us to that understanding. Then, naturally, we have respect for the true source, Sangye Tönpa Shenrab, who taught this wisdom of Yungdrung Bön.

All of these—the teaching, the teacher, the lineage masters, and the Enlightened Ones—are connected. We normally say everything in this life and everything that is existing is interdependent. That is the concept and philosophy. Everything is interconnected. Nothing in relative existence is independent. Everything depends on other things. For a flower to blossom, a seed is not enough. It needs sun, water, and soil. In this way, everything is interdependent.

We need to think about this not only on the level of knowledge and understanding, but also on the level of realization and experience. To understand and have respect for the teaching, we must respect the teaching essence. This provides the benefit in our experience.

Beginning with this first stanza, we should appreciate that we have met this very teaching of Bön. Ask yourself: *Why is this teaching important? Why are the teachings the source of my true happiness?* Ask yourself this and get a satisfactory answer. Keep this sense of wonder and curiosity with you throughout your day. Contemplate deeply. If you can think that the teachings are the source of happiness, you should also have a reason for why it is the source.

Most everyone's goal in life is to be truly happy. So, reflect on this. *What makes you practice? What makes you want to learn about Bön?*

II

Commitment

2. Commitment

གཉིས་བཅའ་བ་ནི།
Second, commitment:

ཕན་བདེའི་འབྱུང་གནས་སངས་རྒྱས་སེམས་དཔའ་ཡི།
The source of benefit and happiness is the Enlightened Ones and Sempas (Warm-hearted Ones).

ཉམས་རྟོགས་ལས་བྱུང་དེ་ཡང་རང་གི་སེམས།
It also comes from experiencing and realizing one's natural mind.

རྟོགས་དང་མ་རྟོགས་གཉིས་ལ་རགས་ལུས་པས།
Because it depends on realizing or not realizing,

དེ་བས་རང་སེམས་ཡང་དག་རྟོགས་པར་བྱ།
I will therefore realize my own ultimate mind.

The first line of this stanza is talking about our happiness and being of benefit to others. It is saying the source of these qualities are the Enlightened Ones (Sangye) and the Warm-hearted Ones (Sempa).

The Enlightened Ones are fully accomplished. They have the full capacity to manifest their wisdom and compassion anywhere. Similarly, the Warm-hearted Ones are always full of compassion for other beings, even those that act wrongly toward them. In their compassion, they work tirelessly for all sentient beings. These two types of beings have great capacity for spreading happiness and benefit. They have realized the ultimate reality of their own Nature of Mind and have gone beyond ignorance and all emotion. They understand both the mind and the Nature of Mind.

This second stanza is the master's own advice and his commitment. It is saying that the source of happiness is within; it is carried within us. We need to discover it—to realize it.

Where is this source? Where is it coming from? It is coming from their unconditional love and compassion, as well the realizations of the Enlightened Ones and highly realized masters.

What is being realized? Our own mind. It is teaching us that all the sources of happiness and sorrow of the individual and of the whole world is connected directly to our own mind. This means that when we realize our own mind and its nature, we can gradually become free from attachment and ignorance by cutting the root of ignorance—the root of suffering within cyclic existence.

When we don't realize the sources of suffering, then we are deluded, meaning that we are not finding the path to free ourselves from suffering. We are still in the same cycle, the same situation as everyone else, and are therefore suffering.

Every experience—joy, pleasure, happiness, or suffering—is related to our own mind and its perception. All the sources of happiness, as well as unhappiness, are connected to our mind. Our mind manifests as positive activities or qualities, or negative activities that disturb our inner peace and the quality of our experience.

So here, His Holiness Sonam Lodrö instructs that because the source of everything is our own mind, we should put our energy into realizing that very mind—to find our own self by discovering it as it truly is. Therefore, he says, "practice to discover the true nature of your mind" and quotes from the *Prajnaparamita* text, saying that the differences between our cyclic existence and the Enlightened Ones is only realizing or not realizing our own true Nature of Mind.

When we realize our mind as it is, we have no reason to be deluded or mistaken. There is no reason to have wrong understanding. For example, if we know a person well, then we will not mistake that person for someone else, because we clearly recognize and know them. In the same way, when we realize our true Nature of Mind, we recognize it, and we realize it as clear, perfect, and free from suffering. Realization is like a moon arising in a cloudless sky—bright, clear, exact, and perfect.

When we don't realize the true nature of phenomena, we begin to manifest whatever we have wrongly conceptualized. This illusion is manifested only because of a lack of understanding of who we are, as we are. So, the instruction here is to put focus on realizing who we are.

His Holiness is also stating that he is watching and looking at himself, at the nature of his own mind. He is making a self-commitment to put effort to understand and realize the true nature of his own mind.

True wisdom, compassion, happiness, and benefit to others will depend on whether we understand and realize our own Nature of Mind or not.

COMMITMENT

The difference between sentient beings and the Enlightened Ones is not really a big gap. It is simply whether we understand the truth or not. All our actions are based on what we understand or don't understand. If we follow what we don't understand, the rest of our actions will also be based on projections and illusions.

The source of everything is based on whether we realize our own true Nature of Mind. So, make the commitment, make the effort, spend the time, and practice.

In this stanza, His Holiness is making a commitment that he will not allow his conventional mind to engage in ignorance or emotion, which leads to suffering. He is making a commitment to always try to watch his Nature or Mind and to be mindful of his conscious thoughts.

On one level, he is emphasizing the relative or conditional level of how to be compassionate and open-hearted for all sentient beings—to not have a self-centered focus but a focus on benefitting the wellbeing of others.

Ultimately, he is emphasizing realizing our mind, which is none other than the emptiness of clarity—clear light that is empty, open, and spacious. It is not empty like nothingness; it is spacious in that it is open space, full of the qualities of compassion, kindness, and love.

This is something you can focus on today. Watch yourself on a relative level, and then also on a deeper level, in essence, to see the true nature or reality of your mind.

Begin by making a self-commitment to watch yourself today. Keep that commitment.

Let your body and mind relax and be open for meditation. Put effort to watch your thought, which is always present in the body, in the brain, in the heart—the so-called "thought" that exists in the body. This "neutral thought" is why we normally keep thinking, so without thinking of anything specifically, just be in the presence of watching that neutral thought. Watch it without following it, without going ahead, and without remaining behind. Just be in the presence of watching. Simply remain there in that presence.

Remember this commitment to watch your mind time to time throughout your day. Remember what you're thinking and how you're thinking while in the process of thinking. What are you able to identify? Are you able to see who is thinking? Who is making decisions as they are made in your day? In what way is your thought responding or reacting?

Remember your commitment to watch the mind, the thought that is your "self." Watch yourself as you are able throughout the day, and then during your practice in the morning or evening, watch it closely during mediation.

III

Preliminaries

3. Making a Meaningful Life

གསུམ་པ་སྟོན་འགྲོ་ལ་བདུན།
Third, the seven preliminaries:

དང་པོ་དལ་འབྱོར་དོན་ཡོད་བྱ་བ་ནི།
First, making a meaningful life:

ཇི་ལྟར་དཀའ་བ་ཡིད་བཞིན་ནོར་བུ་འདྲ།
Just as it is as rare to find wish fulfilling gems,

དལ་འབྱོར་མི་ལུས་རིན་ཆེན་ཐོབ་དུས་འདིར།
[So is] the achievement of a perfect and precious human body in this life.

རང་གཞན་འཁོར་བའི་རྒྱ་མཚོར་བསྒྲལ་བའི་ཕྱིར།
In order to liberate both self and others from the ocean of cyclic existence,

ཉིན་མཚན་ཀུན་ཏུ་ཡེངས་མེད་སེམས་ལ་ལྟ།
Without distraction, I look to the mind both day and night.

This section begins the third part of the text. After the Verse of Praise and the Commitment, we are now beginning with the preliminary teachings. There are seven parts to the preliminaries, this being the first.

This stanza tells us how to make our life meaningful. It says that having a human body, a human life, is rare. In future lifetimes, we may not have a body. Even if we have a human form, we may not have the right condition or situation that allows us to receive and practice the teachings. We may even be unable to do good for other sentient beings. But having this opportunity now is like finding a precious gem—what we call a *wish-fulfilling gem*. In Tibetan teachings, it says that if one finds a wish-fulfilling jewel or gem, and one prays for what is wished for, that wish will be granted.

This teaching tells us that this present human body is as precious and as rare as wish-fulfilling gems. Like one of these gems, in this human life, we can achieve anything we wish, but we must put energy toward it. We must work to manifest it.

How do we make this precious life more meaningful and not waste this rare opportunity? How do we make ourselves feel like we have had a meaningful day? We can do this by helping others. When we make someone else happy or protect them in a situation, we feel good. It may give us the sense that we can liberate or free sentient beings from suffering. But even if we have the desire to free others from their suffering and misery, we usually continue to do things that lead us to repeating our cyclic existence. If we don't help to free others from their suffering, it is like having wish-fulfilling jewels and not using them. What is the use of having wisdom and not sharing it? The text is saying that we have the potential to do good, so we mustn't waste it; we must make our human lives meaningful.

How do we make our life truly meaningful? We do so by helping other sentient beings by giving them minor joy, peace, happiness, and comfort. But the text is saying that ultimately, in order to maximize the help to sentient beings, we must improve our own spiritual quality by realizing our true Nature of Mind. By understanding the importance of our own practice and training, we are able to manifest our full potential so that we can help and liberate other sentient beings.

It is not going to happen in a day, a week, or a year, but we must practice in every moment, keeping that thought always present in the mind.

At any moment, we can become instruments to help other beings, even in minor things. Simply our willingness to help others generates an inner quality and energy that grows stronger over time. Through inner growth, we can be a model for others. Our actions of the body, the ways we speak, our thoughts—they all become directed toward the benefit and happiness of others.

In day-to-day life, many of my students are engaged in helping others—giving support and being involved in social works that benefit many people in their community or elsewhere. This is part of practice in action.

In daily life, there can always be practice in action. If we can keep that in our awareness, we don't need a specific time or place to practice.

First, we must think positive thoughts. Then, we change our speech into good speech—even saying a single word that makes someone happy. And then there is action of body. We do something to bring comfort to others, giving them joy and happiness.

This is a practical, down-to-earth way of engaging in practice daily. It allows for the quality of practice to grow. Gradually, it awakens us inside. Eventually, we no longer need any kind of forceful thought. We no longer must tell ourselves to do good deeds, to practice, or to be a good person. It becomes habitual and spontaneous.

With a strong foundation in practice, we will not generate negative, evil, or harmful thoughts toward others. That is why we say to make a life of practice. Our whole life should be practice. Some think that if we just meditate five or ten minutes in the morning, then we are a practitioner. That is better than nothing, but we can do much more.

The main point of this stanza is to enthusiastically integrate our day-to-day life into practice in order to improve the quality of our spirituality. Then, we will have a meaningful life.

At the same time, as we cultivate positivity, we also should put energy into decreasing negative thoughts, actions, and speech. Realize when actions are harming others, recognize it, and try not to do it again. That is the practice.

Reciting Nyenpas (Skt. Mantras) and saying prayers of the Yidam in the morning and then doing negative actions the rest of the day, doesn't make sense. Searching for peace while engaging in violence or creating problems for others don't go together. If we are truly searching for real happiness, we need to realize that others want the same quality of happiness.

If we live only 20 years, but we have been able to do something good for ourselves and others, our life has been worthwhile. If we live 70 or 80 years but have never done anything to create happiness for others—and rather have always been destructive, unpleasant, or a disturbance—then our life has no meaning or quality. Our life is not fulfilled when we are just breathing and moving. We are only fulfilled when we have made life meaningful.

We often don't realize how fortunate we are, simply because we're experiencing struggles. When we are in this cyclic world called *khorwa* (cyclic existence), there is no way to expect everything to be perfect without challenges. Challenge itself is a part of life.

But we are in a position of opportunity while we have this precious life. We need to make it something special and fulfilling so that we can feel proud and happy that we have used our life in a productive way.

In the higher teachings of Dzogchen, it says that when we truly develop inner realization, then it doesn't matter whether we are eating, sleeping, sitting, or moving; during all four of these times, we still can remain in an awareness of realization. We must train our mind to always remain in the presence of our meditation. We integrate our practice into the action of day-to-day life. Then the practice itself is always there, and life becomes meaningful.

Even with practice, in our daily life, there may be moments when we are happy or moments when we are unhappy, but we will still be okay. We recognize the next moment could be happy or unhappy. We know nothing is constant or reliable. This moment of happiness can in one hour become sorrow. There is nothing we can rely on. The only thing we can rely on is the discovering of our true self-realization, the true Nature of Mind.

Doing so liberates us, freeing us from the pain of existence, from the cause of suffering.

So, observe yourself in every single moment, at all hours, both day and night, being always present within yourself.

Early on, even when meditating, practitioners are often not mindfully present. Even if the body is in meditation posture and one begins with the motive of quality meditation, once they enter a meditation, they're not always present. So, make the effort and self-commitment to watch your own Nature of Mind. Even when you go to the washroom, be in the presence of yourself. Even when you are having a coffee together with friends and everyone is talking and gossiping, be aware you're gossiping. Don't let yourself get completely lost in the gossiping. As always, awareness is very important. Be aware; be present.

The teaching points inside. The teaching never takes us away from ourselves. It is meant to point at us. Be aware of that. Then we don't need effort to get where we want to go, because we are already there.

Time to time, think to yourself. Do you really value your precious life? Do you think your life is precious?

Human life is very precious and rare. It provides a great opportunity, being the result of positive past karma and merit. Consider how much you are valuing it and making it worthwhile.

Additionally, consider how often you are present within yourself. Work to remember and reflect throughout the day. Bring yourself within your body and be present until you're fully content.

4. Eliminating the Source of the Three Poisons

གཉིས་པ་དུག་གསུམ་འབྱུང་གཞི་ཕ་ཡུལ་སྤངས་པ་ནི།

Second, abandoning one's fatherland, the source of the three poisons:

གཉེན་གྱི་ཕྱོགས་ལ་འདོད་ཆགས་ཆུ་ལྟར་ཁོལ།

Attachment to friends and relatives is like water boiling.

དགྲ་ཡི་ཕྱོགས་ལ་ཞེ་སྡང་མེ་ལྟར་འབར།

Anger toward enemies is like a blazing fire.

སྤང་བླང་བརྗེད་པའི་གཏི་མུག་མུན་ལྟར་འཐིབས།

Closed-mindedness (timug) darkens the [faculties of] rejection and acceptance like a thick fog.

ཕ་ཡུལ་སྤངས་ནས་དགེ་རྩ་བརྟན་པ་ཡིན།

By abandoning the fatherland, the root of virtue is grounded.

This fourth stanza tells us that is of vital importance to reject the sources of the three poisons. If we are attached to relatives or others who are close to us, it is like water that is boiling. Anger towards an enemy or one we dislike is comparable to a fire's flames. Our closed mindedness (*timug*) fully covers our knowledge, inhibiting our ability to distinguish between right and wrong. But, if we can detach from our fatherland or homeland, we can be well-grounded in virtuous qualities.

We are most attached to relatives and people we feel close to. We ignore those we don't know, and we easily feel anger toward those we think of as enemies or people we dislike.

If good things happen to our family and friends, it is easy for us to react with inner happiness and participate in their happiness. And if something goes wrong in their lives, we also easily participate in their sorrow and unhappiness. We are sometimes so totally and deeply attached to them that we hold on to them as if we were glued to them.

However, if those same things happen to someone we don't know, we may have different feelings or be less concerned one way or another. Additionally, if something bad happens to someone we dislike or who we feel is an enemy, we may feel good. We may even feel uplifted because something went wrong for a person we don't like.

The example for attachment is like boiling water. When we boil water on the stove, there is a fire under it. If the fire stays lit, the water keeps bubbling endlessly. This is like attachment. Attachment creates more attachment. We must learn to let it go—to release it rather than holding onto it.

The more we hold on, the more we want to hold on. We continue holding, and even if we think we need to release the object of our attachment, we are unable to because we have become too deeply attached. Therefore, attachment can sometimes be said to cause the other poisons. Because of attachment, we can kill, we might steal, or we may unknowingly act ignorantly. While ignorance is the root poison, attachment can also lead to other poisons like anger, hatred, jealously, and so on.

Anger is like a fire flame. Anything put into fire will burn up; it will be destroyed. While we can run away from external fire, we cannot run away from our inner fire because we carry it with us. It burns us from within. Our attachment can add to the anger, like throwing dry wood on it.

These first two poisons occur because of ignorance, the third poison. This stanza gives an example of ignorance as a thick fog covering our wisdom. Thick fog prevents us from seeing into the distance or seeing things clearly, as they truly are. This ignorance, when energized, may manifest as anger, attachment, hatred, jealously, etc.

The text is saying that we are living our day-to-day life with attachment, with anger, with ignorance, and with all the negativity that comes with them. We know these poisons are not good, and we don't enjoy acting in these ways, but when the poisons manifest, we forget how to control them. We don't even remember that we are supposed to control each of these energies when they arise. So, through our ignorance, we keep allowing these energies to manifest. Our inner ignorance gives us the energy to allow these other negative energies, and in some ways, we may even think they are good for us.

When we get angry with someone, we use harsh language or act violently. In these cases, we often think we are protecting ourselves. But we are damaging, destroying, and disturbing ourselves. In the same way, when we have attachment towards someone close to us, we may take their side because we may not be able to see the fault in their side. This blind attachment can cause us to add to the problem, which can lead to further problems, violence, or destruction.

Therefore, these stanzas teach us how important it is to be truthful with mental clarity, and to not fall into the emotional side of ignorance. Stay in the middle without taking sides. Look at both sides honestly. Try to learn and understand the real situation, before making a decision based in truth. If you want to take a side in a situation, stand with the truth.

We need to train our mind in this way. The truth is: there is no side. We take sides because of our ignorance. We may think there is a side to choose, but there is no side. We should work to realize this. Look at it carefully and try to apply this realization. At the very beginning, it may be very inconvenient. Our friends or relatives may think we are ignoring, disregarding, or disrespecting them. But the more we learn not to take sides unnecessarily, the more strength, confidence, and comfort we will feel in not falling on one side or another in every argument.

Sooner or later, there will be a moment of joy and achievement. First, you may go through great challenges with your close friends and relatives, because they may disagree with you. But by standing up for the truth, they will ultimately appreciate it and be happy in the end. However, if we only try to ease and please others regardless of the reality of the situation, while those people may have temporary joy, in the end, everyone will suffer and regret it.

We should look at the long-term benefit and achievement—true happiness. True happiness will never be experienced by doing wrong or by unnecessarily taking sides.

There are many who are very sectarian, and they promote the sectarian attitudes of their community with disturbances and violence. The result is unhappiness for everyone.

Spiritual or religious teachings should bring things together rather than dividing them. It should be like glue. If things are broken, we use glue to fix them. Bön teachings talk about this. We see what makes things distinct. Then we try our best—honestly and genuinely—to bring them together.

Don't worry about whether people like your decision or not. Don't choose just to make people temporarily happy. If you choose wrong, in the end, people will dislike you when they discover the truth. We must learn how to calculate the long-term benefit versus temporarily making a situation peaceful.

No matter how thick the clouds cover the horizon, the sunlight is not totally covered. In time, the clouds will move, and the sun will show its true brightness. It takes time. We need patience. But we should not take a side if it is not true or honest. Be on the side of truth. That is the point.

In the final line of the stanza, it says that if we renounce or leave our fatherland, then we are grounded in spiritual quality. What does this mean? After living and growing up in our own birthplace, that place is like the physical root of ourselves. This great connection to the land can lead us to engage in various kinds of attachment, anger, or ignorance. We may feel the need to agree with the preferences of our father or relatives. If our father dislikes someone, should we be closed off to that person? Does he have a reasonable reason? Or does he simply dislike the person because of his own ignorance, or because of his anger, or because of his attachment to personal gain? If we blindly follow the preferences of our father—or the preferences of those that live in our community—without considering the truth of the situation, this does not make us a good, honest person.

Staying in our homeland gives us more conditions and opportunity to generate anger toward those our relatives dislike. It also grants us more access to attachment because we are always surrounded with all the conditions of attachment—we have more access to it. Once we are far away and in someplace new, we have less conditions for anger, attachment, and ignorance to arise. When we are somewhere totally new, we have much less reason to take sides in our family's worldly struggles, preferences, and prejudices. Without having to choose a side, we are automatically free from these potentially poisonous conditions.

We should also consider that, by leaving, we may be avoiding issues in our fatherland. Some may say they are leaving to avoid conditions for poisons to arise, but they are running away to avoid problems. It may be better for some to try to stay and develop their mind, and therefore not have the need to run away.

We must know that no matter how far we go away from our homeland, in time we will create more friends and more enemies, and we will be expected to make the same choices of liking or disliking someone or something. The process of conceptual grasping, choices, and falling on one side of things will repeat again automatically. Will you run away again? How many times will you run away?

Here the text means that, conditionally or temporarily, leaving one's fatherland can help us to reduce our poisons. But while it may help us temporarily, we must truly develop ourselves—our realization that thought-grasping and taking sides is essence-less. Instead, we need to learn not to take sides, which develops habits and clinging in this cyclic existence and rather, practice generating loving kindness for those we feel anger toward, or people we disagree with.

The answer is to generate self-realization. This is a wisdom to overcome ignorance. When we do that, we don't have to run away. Running away is only a temporary method that can help us initially stabilize ourselves without constant conditions for poisons. But it is not an absolute method. It shows us how to temporarily avoid things, but we cannot truly avoid them unless we can change our inner view and look at situations without taking a side.

5. Hermitage, the Source of Inner Qualities

གསུམ་པ་དབེན་གནས་བསྟེན་པ་ནི།

Third, the hermitage, the source of good qualities:

ཉེ་རིང་ཆགས་སྡང་མ་ལུས་དབྲལ་བའི་ཕྱིར།

In order to detach from both attachment and aversion towards those near and far,

ཤིན་ཏུ་དབེན་པའི་གནས་མཆོག་བསྟེན་གྱུར་ན།

If I can make use of a very quiet and isolated sacred place,

རང་སེམས་དགའ་བའི་བག་སྒྲིབ་བྱད་གྱུར་ཅིག

I wish to develop a joyous state of mind and exhaust my [karmic] obscurations.

ཡོན་ཏན་ཡར་ངོའི་ཟླ་ལྟར་འཕེལ་བར་འགྱུར།

May inner qualities increase like the month's waxing moon.

If one lives in the quietness of complete solitude, they will cultivate happiness within and remove any karmic desecrations. In such a state, one can expel attachment and anger that is projected towards others. This is referring to the temporal and material condition of our self-quietness and peacefulness. When we are too sensitive, it is easy to feel distracted. Quietness can be a good support. In the beginning, when we are learning to meditate, even barking dogs bother our focus. When we develop stability of focus, the neighbor's dog won't be a bother. Even mediating in an airport or train station may not bother us.

Because the bother is not from outside; the bother is from inside. If we are developing ourselves to not be bothered by surrounding external conditions, we are building up strength inside.

At the very beginning, we are like an unstable feather on top of a windy pass. When the wind comes, the feather cannot choose to remain there; the wind takes it away. When we develop inner strength and stability, we become more like a solid iron ball or rock—even a mountain. No matter how strong the wind blows, we remain stable, like nothing has happened. When we have that stability inside us, we don't need to run away.

But being in the quietness of a hermitage gives us temporary inner joy, peace, and quiet, which supports us in having a normal and harmonious state of experience. Like going to a beautiful garden or a dense forest, where there are waterfalls, different bird sounds, and wind in the leaves. All these things give us a sense of pleasure, a feeling of joy, happiness, and quietness. We feel relaxed and calm. That is the symbol of our inner potential for true calm, happiness, and quiet.

But we do not experience this very clearly and actively in everyday life because we are so distracted. If we have access to remote places and hermitages, going there to practice helps by letting us settle into our true state of peace. This is helping and conditioning us, but it is not a true discovery of happiness.

Therefore, it says that if we live there in a hermitage, we have no friends to be attached to. We have no enemies to be angry with. We have no one around to generate jealously. We have no one whom we disregard or disrespect. We are alone, surrounded only by nature, whose energy and quality we begin adopting within. We begin to experience more inner joy, inner happiness, and inner quiet.

At a certain point, we discover our true self nature, the true face of happiness, the true face of clarity, our own natural state of mind. And then we continue to discover and experience. That is how we advance our inner wisdom.

We must work with both of these conditions—when things are quiet, as well as the distractive, hectic society and samsaric, material world. It can be so distracting, and we can be so completely driven into it, we might hardly think about how to get out of it.

The hermitage is more constructive, while being in society and in the community is more distracting. Try to find those places that will help you to discover the ultimate quietness.

Going to the wilderness is not the ultimate solution; it is a temporal condition to help you discover the ultimate true understanding. Day-to-day, if we keep these qualities in our thoughts, we automatically help ourselves inwardly, without needing to go to a hermitage in the wilderness.

It's not always possible to go to a hermitage. In that case, we also must be able to discover our true Nature of Mind while being in society, because we are born in society. Living in a wilderness may be beneficial to our own growth and practice, but we can still achieve those qualities while in society. We should try to be beneficial in the society in which we are connected.

If you cannot go to a hermitage, then mix into society. Put your practice into action in the society. Make whatever contribution you can in a positive way. That is the essence of practice.

6. Following the Lama, the Source of Blessings

བཞི་པ་བྱིན་རླབས་འབྱུང་གནས་བླ་མ་བསྟེན་པ་ནི།

Fourth, following the Lama, the source of blessings:

བདག་ནི་བླ་མ་དམ་པ་རྟག་བརྟེན་པའི།

I always depend on the precious Lama.

བླ་མའི་ཐུགས་རྗེས་རྒྱུན་དུ་བཟུང་བའི་མཐུས།

By the power of being held in the Lama's continuous compassion,

རང་རོ་སྟོད་པའི་བྱིན་རླབས་སྒྲོན་མེ་ཡིས།

Whose power of introducing self-realization is the blessing like a lamp

རང་སེམས་མུན་པའི་སྒོ་བརྒྱ་འབྱེད་པར་བྱེད།

That open hundreds of doors [illuminating] the darkness of my own mind.

This stanza is about our relationship with the teacher and how the teacher is important to our practice and our spiritual life. This includes both keeping our outer body, speech, and mind connected by receiving teachings, as well as keeping the teacher in our heart in every moment—the inner connection. A genuine inner connection is essential to spiritual development and to one's realization of the ultimate nature of all phenomena.

This stanza explains that we should always follow the teacher. That doesn't mean we should go wherever they are teaching or follow their worldly life. The true meaning of following the teacher is to understand them better and feel comfortable accepting and following their teachings—applying those teachings both in practice and in day-to-day life.

We do not need to be always present with our teacher physically, unless it is to receive teachings, etc. To follow the teacher means to be able to benefit from his or her wisdom and knowledge by showing them respect and putting the practices to use in this life, making changes for the better.

All the Sangyes of the past have followed the essence and instruction taught by their teachers. The original source of the teachings goes back to Sangye Tönpa Shenrab, but because we don't have the good fortune to receive the teachings directly from him, we learn the messages he left through our teachers. Even though our teachers are human beings, we should view them positively—as a form of the enlightened Sangye. Their speech, knowledge, and qualities of minds are the same as the Enlightened Ones. We should not see our teacher as just a regular person, but as the enlightened qualities that they represent.

In the A-tri Ngöndro, the nine preliminary practices, we visualize the teacher in Lamai Naljor. We either visualize them as Shenlha Wökar or as Tapihritsa above us. This is the teacher's mind essence; it is no different than the essence of the Sangye of Compassion. Because of that, we receive the quality, power, blessing, and wisdom of the Sangye.

The inner quality of the master is meant to be equal to or inseparable from the quality of the Sangye. If we look at the teacher as the same as ourselves, then there is nothing we can expect from them other than just the words of an ordinary human being. When we transform our view toward the Lama—his or her body, speech, and mind—then we will be able to experience something we ordinarily cannot. In this way, the teaching and teacher are part of the path transforming us internally. This is how we keep the teacher in our mind.

We receive these teachings through our Lama, just as he or she received them through their masters. In this way, an unbroken lineage is transmitted. The Lama is carrying and preserving that lineage, quality, and tradition so that it can be transmitted to you.

Sangye Tönpa Shenrab will not come to us and explain the teachings. We have no capacity to connect with him at this moment. He has been gone for 18,000 years. But his teachings, blessings, and their qualities still exist. We receive these through our teacher who is connected to it. What we learn and discover within ourselves is transmitted from that master. Because of this, we don't look at our master like a professor at the university. Instead, there is a deeper connection inside that opens our true wisdom.

While a secular teacher gives us external knowledge, the Lama helps us see our true nature. They point out to us who we really are—the nature of our own mind.

Even having the texts of the complete oral teaching of Sangye Tönpa Shenrab, all 178 volumes, will not give us the true essence and meaning unless a teacher explains it and transmits the connection to his own masters and the lineage going all the way back to the origin.

This stanza is teaching us to value the wisdom and knowledge of teachers, while at the same time showing us a path to keep the teacher preciously by trying to follow his or her guidance and applying it in our life. If we can do this, then we can receive the blessings in the form of wisdom and realization.

It is like when we light a lamp in a dark room, and it lets us see the objects in the room. This is the wisdom and blessing of the teaching and of the masters. This wisdom protects us from ignorance and from sinking into cyclic existence, into khorwa. It helps us distinguish ignorance from wisdom and to see and remove obstacles to the practice. It supports us in generating compassion and helps us realize the true Nature of Mind. This all comes from the teacher.

The teacher is a messenger of Sangye Tönpa Shenrab and of earlier masters. We teachers are freshly transmitting it to students, and through the students' understanding, it is eliminating their negative karma. Elimination of negative karma means cleansing the darkness of ignorance with knowledge and wisdom. This removes the obstacles we are carrying. By understanding the potential of the teaching of Bön, and applying that in the practice, it automatically begins reducing and removing negative karma, establishing mental clarity, positive qualities, and good merit.

Gaining in the two merits of method and wisdom (*thab* and *sherab* respectively) is part of the ten transcendental practices. It automatically opens the 100 dark doors of ignorance. When we have the light of wisdom inside us, there is no place for the darkness of ignorance. These two can't be in the same place at the same time. Our practice is meant to be like a lamp of inner wisdom and knowledge, which is only possible through the teacher's explanations.

This is why we always practice daily prayers. To open our eyes and generate a good attitude and motivation, we recite the supplication prayer of Nyammed Sherab Gyaltsen. He is known as the root teacher of Bön, the source of all the lineage of all the teachings. Every one of us is connected to our root teacher. Each of our root teachers is connected to their own root teachers, and if you keep going back to the 14th century, you will come to realize most authentic sources of lineage are connected to Gyalwa Nyipa Nyammed Sherab Gyaltsen, (Gyalwa Nyam Medpa) from whom all teaching lineages were transmitted.

Therefore, in every Bönpo community, Nyammed Sherab Gyaltsen's birthday and enlightenment anniversaries are celebrated. In any Bönpo monastery or group anywhere, in any country, no matter whether lay practitioners or monk, every prayer session starts with Nyammed Sherab Gyaltsen's invocation prayer.

So, remember, the distance to the teacher doesn't matter; the place doesn't matter. It is the true quality of devotion and faith in him or her that matters. Our level of effort determines how well we can connect with our teacher through practice. The teaching is meant to make us a more genuine person.

We should not change our attitude of respect toward the teachings, the Sangye, or the teacher. If we have a true understanding of the value of the connection to them, then whether we are comfortable and joyful or whether we are going through a terrible problem, we remain connected. The more we connect, the more we are present for the blessing of protection and guidance.

Follow the teacher correctly and properly. Don't change the concept toward the teacher every moment like the weather, or you will never receive any qualities or benefits. This is very important. This is not my idea but is as past masters have said. So, hold the teacher as a precious jewel. Carry that potential for wisdom, quality, and essence wherever you are.

7. Entering the Path of Virtue

ལྔ་པ་ཐར་ལམ་འབྱུང་གནས་དགེ་ལ་འཇུག་པ་ནི།
Fifth, entering into virtue, the origin of the path of liberation:

ཐར་ལམ་དུ་སླུ་སྒྲུར་དུ་བགྲོད་པའི་ཕྱིར།
In order to travel the path of liberation, at this moment,

འདི་ནས་བྱང་ཆུབ་སྙིང་པོ་མ་ཐོབ་པར།
From now on, until attaining the essence of enlightenment,

མི་དགེ་སྡིག་པ་གཅིག་ཀྱང་མི་བྱེད་ཅིང་།
[I] will not do even one unwholesome action, and

དགེ་བའི་ཡོན་ཏན་ཕུན་སུམ་འཚོགས་པར་བྱ།
Will collect the accomplishments of quality and virtue.

This stanza talks about how we enter into the path of practice.

Begin by considering: What makes you think you are a practitioner? What makes you think you are Bön or Buddhist?

If we are carrying the potential of Bön or Buddhist teachings, and we are living the teachings as much as we can—mentally, physically, and verbally—and if the teachings influence our actions, thoughts, and speech—then we are connected with Bön.

We live our lives based on our trust and faith in the Sangye, the Bön teaching, and the Yungdrung Sempa. Living our lives with their positive influence and doing virtuous deeds will generate comfort, joy, and positive merit within us. Understand that doing non-virtuous deeds conditions us to go through unpleasant experiences, including unhappiness, disturbances, and unfriendliness.

Think of how you speak to others. Make the commitment to say things that will make other people calm. Speak the truth, be genuine, don't use harsh language, don't gossip, and don't tell lies. Keep these things in mind and avoid these negative actions of speech as much as you can.

If you cannot control your negative speech, try to realize it immediately. Make the commitment not to repeat it. If you can live while holding this concept of right speech, you are in the practice; you are on the path of practice. By doing this, your practice gradually develops.

If you are totally thoughtless and don't pay attention to how your speech can hurt others, if you think wrongly or negatively, if your body action is wild, rough, or violent—and you do not put your attention to recognizing these negativities—you are being influenced more and more by those negative deeds.

Negative deeds and positive deeds have two different levels of energies that function or circle in your body. They affects your breathing, your body's channels, your energy points (Skt. *chakras*), your pulse and nerves—your entire body and mind. By training your body, speech, and mind, you can calm yourself. Work to engage in this. Think carefully before you speak.

Language is the bridge between ourselves and others. By changing the way we speak, we help others to have a better, more positive experience. Our manner of speaking makes connections with other people. Using harsh language does not create an inner positive connection. It often only pushes others away. Using soft and genuine speech gives pleasure to others, brings them closer together, makes situations friendlier, and creates strong bridges.

Be mindful of yourself in your day-to-day actions. A lack of awareness and mindfulness leads to wrongdoing. By being mindful, we encourage ourselves to do good deeds and create a positive effect. When we realize we are doing good actions and are gaining the result of these good actions, it encourages us to go further.

In the same way, when we realize we are doing negative deeds, realizing that they are not correct discourages us from repeating them. This way, our mindfulness protects us from creating negative karma and negative energies.

Mindfulness is something that is essential in practice and in day-to-day life. In Tibetan, we call it *Drenpa dang Shezhin* which means the internal watchfulness that we need to guide us and guard us from these wrong qualities.

So, each and every moment, engage in virtuous deeds. Even the intention of wanting to do good deeds for everyone, and praying for good things to happen to all people, increases our inner qualities. When we improve our actions of body, speech, and mind, gradually we become more and more purified, cleansed, and free from all negatives. We can experience more of the positive qualities. We will feel more joy, happiness, and positivity.

Be mindful to perform virtuous deeds, engaging every moment in acts like circumambulation, praying in the morning and evening, and reflecting on the essence of the teachings.

Look at yourself. How much of the time are you in practice, and how much are you not in practice within a day? How many times do you think of practice? How many times do you think of positive deeds? How much of the time do you think of negative deeds? Check yourself. Then, you'll see where still you need to improve.

8. Practice on Impermanence

དྲུག་པ་འཁོར་བ་ལ་ཞེན་པ་སྤོག་པའི་ཐབས་མི་རྟག་པ་ཤེས་པར་བྱ་བ་ནི།

Sixth, to extinguish the attachment of cyclic existence, know the method of impermanence:

འཁོར་བའི་བོན་ནི་རྒྱ་ཆེ་གྲངས་མང་པ།

The existence of the cyclic world has countless [aspects] and vast [capacity].

ཐམས་ཅད་མི་རྟག་སྒྱུ་མའི་རང་བཞིན་ལ།

Naturally, all is impermanent and illusionary—

རང་གི་སྤོག་ལུས་དབང་ཐང་ལོངས་སྤྱོད་ལ།

All wealth, power, body senses, and one's own life.

ཆགས་འཛིན་སྤངས་ནས་མི་རྟག་རྒྱུན་དུ་སྒོམས།

Meditate continuously on impermanence and release grasping on [these] desires.

This stanza's advice is to detach and meditate on the impermanence of cyclic existence.

No matter how vast or beautiful we think the material world is, cyclic existence is temporal, changeable, damageable, dissolvable, and destroyable. It only momentarily exists, and there is nothing solid contained within. It is all impermanent.

Why should we practice impermanence? Because we tend to feel strongly inside that life is as it appears to be—everlasting and permanent. In life, we have a strong feeling that it will last forever. But it will not. Nothing that we are connected with physically or materially will last forever. Nothing is solid or everlasting, even though we still grasp at it as everlasting. In Tibetan we call it *dag zin*, meaning "self-grasping," or holding on to things as everlasting—not having a concept of impermanence or understanding life as limited.

We make plans for the future and think about what's going to happen next year at this time. We plan everything ahead as if it's going to last forever. We don't have a sense of the temporal—of momentary existence. If we had that, it would be much easier on us, relieving us of the concept of holding on. Instead, we are always increasing the grasping—self-grasping, grasping on material things, on our relatives, and so on. We are always holding on, thinking of everything as solid and permanent. This perception is far from the way things really are. Impermanence shows us how to look inside and understand how temporary life is. There is nothing in the material world we can always grasp. It is all temporal. It doesn't matter how big something is, eventually it will collapse. In the end, it will be dissolved and destroyed.

On an ordinary day, when we look into our own physical bodies, we sometimes seem so healthy. We feel we are still young. We don't think we are going to die today or next week. We think that our health is good, so we plan to live another 50 years. It's possible this is true, but we shouldn't hold on to that.

If we watch a stage performance at the theater, we will enjoy the show while it is happening. We will have a good time, a good experience, but we don't have a sense of holding onto it. We know it is just a performance. In a larger sense, we must realize that all of life is a performance that is performed by our ignorance and karmic energy. Our relation to the world is usually different than to that of a drama on stage. We must come to know that our whole life is the performance of the drama. If we realize in this way, it decreases our ego and self-centered concept of holding.

Understanding this gives us encouragement to practice without wasting any time. Time is so valuable. While our health is energetic, we need to apply that energy. We may think we can do something tomorrow, or the next day, or next week, or next year, but everything after this moment is not really ours—it is just a hope.

If we do things in the present, then it is ours. If we rely on the future that is coming, that is hope. It is not guaranteed, so it is not ours. It could be or it could not be. And if it doesn't happen as we plan, we have regret.

We cannot bring the past into the present. We cannot bring the future into the present. We only have the present right now. Take advantage of everything right now without relying on the hope of the future or the regret of the past.

Impermanence is not something to scare us or to make us lose hope. We can always plan; we can always have hope, but we shouldn't have grasping. Grasping is ignorance. It is what blocks the wisdom.

Think of people close to you—your parents and ancestors who are no longer living. They have also lived like us. They all thought the same way as us. But none of them lived permanently. Everyone has passed, and we will as well. And those who come in the future will also leave. The only certainty is that people come and go, come and go. When we deeply realize that everything comes and goes, that means we are confirming our understanding and implementing the essence of this teaching.

Impermanence practice is meant to awaken us. We have no certainty that we will last another day or another hour, so we practice or perform virtuous deeds, and we don't waste an opportunity.

Our life really is an opportunity. If we have qualities that allow us to think about doing good, we can act in a good way. We can bring benefit to others, but only if we act without postponing it. When we are truly awakened, we will not waste a single moment.

9. Going to Refuge in the Four Supreme Objects

བདུན་པ་བསླུ་མེད་གནས་བཞི་ལ་སྐྱབས་སུ་འགྲོ་བ་ནི།

Seventh, going for refuge in the unerring, Four Supreme Objects:

རང་ཡང་འཁོར་བའི་བཙོན་རར་བཅིངས་པ་ཡི།

Our own self is trapped in the prison of the cyclic realm.

འཇིག་རྟེན་ལྷ་ཡིས་སུ་ཞིག་སྐྱོབས་པར་ནུས།

None among the worldly gods are able to protect us.

དེ་ཕྱིར་འཇིགས་སྐྲག་ཀུན་ལས་སྐྱོབ་ནུས་པ།

Therefore, with the ability to protect from every fear and agitation,

ཡུལ་མཆོག་གནས་བཞིན་ཁྱེད་ལ་སྐྱབས་སུ་འཚལ།

We seek refuge in you, the Four Supreme Objects.

The Four Supreme Objects of refuge are the Lama (Teacher); Sangye (Enlightened Ones); Yungdrung Sempa (the Warm-hearted Ones who have achieved the mind of enlightenment, also known as Bodhisattvas in Sanskrit); and Bön (the Teaching itself, known as Dharma in Sanskrit). These Four Supreme Objects have a quality that we can receive benefit from to free ourselves from the suffering of cyclic existence. Sometimes we speak of the Three Jewels (Sangye, Bön teachings, and Sempa), but Bön teachings often add the Lama as the fourth of the Four Supreme Object of Refuge.

This stanza says that one's own self is trapped in the prison of cyclic existence. How can we protect ourselves from such suffering or protect and help others? We need the same level of wisdom, compassion, and realization as the Enlightened Ones. All of us are practicing to gain such qualities, but we don't have them yet. We want to be free from cyclic suffering, but only the Four Supreme Objects have that quality of freedom. The Enlightened Ones have practiced and have reached the stage of enlightenment as a result of their practice. They are free from all faults, negativities, and defilements. They are perfected in all qualities.

A Sangye has the full potential to protect all sentient beings from the suffering of cyclic existence. But we are still suffering here. This is not due to a lack of the Sangye's quality. It is due to our lack of inner faith, trust, and genuine connection to them.

The text says, "if you understand the need to be free from suffering, the only one to go to is the one who is already free from suffering." That is the Sangye, who is already free. We are not asking them to protect us from anything other than the suffering of this cyclic existence.

According to our own ignorance and karmic negativities, we are individually bound by certain conditions of suffering. We need powers ourselves, or we need to seek help from someone else to be free of this suffering. No one who is on the same level as us can protect us from this suffering. We can only protect ourselves by following the path of the teachings of the Enlightened Ones.

There are many worldly protectors and deities. Some people think the worldly protectors can protect them from suffering, and they are fully engaged with worshipping them. But there are two different levels of protectors. One is the enlightened protectors, who are free from suffering, known as "wisdom protectors," or *Yeshe kyi Sungma*. The other protectors are still trapped in cyclic existence themselves, the *Jigten Dregpa*. Even beings in the god realm aren't free from suffering. They are not yet enlightened. They are in a high state and have more quality, energy, and power than us ordinary beings, but they're still not free.

So, to those worldly protectors, we can only ask for help and temporal support—not the protection of an ultimate protector. We can make offerings and ask for their help, praying to them, calling to them. This has some power to help. But these are not the protectors we take refuge in. They are not in a position to protect us from the suffering of cyclic existence, because they themselves are still caught in cyclic existence.

For example, we do the practices of Sidpe Gyalmo, the Queen of Existence, Yeshe Walmo, and Sherab Chamma; these three are three manifestations of one nature. They are wisdom deities—wisdom protectors. They protect as well as guide and liberate us from suffering.

But there are also worldly protectors that offer temporal benefit, rather than ultimate benefit. The text is saying we need to take refuge in the beings who are free from suffering—making sure they are not in the same category as us. The only ones who can protect us from true suffering are the Four Supreme Objects of Refuge. They are always ready to protect and bless us. But we need to call to them and awaken them.

Kongtse Trulgyal was a prince of an island close to Olmo Lung Ring in Tönpa Shenrab's lifetime. He was building a great temple, Sé Khang Karnag Trasal, on the island with the help of many other beings. Because he was a wealthy prince, he wanted to do something special and different that would benefit all sentient beings for a long time. In the middle of a construction project, he was disturbed by evil and wild spirits. They tried to destroy all the buildings that had been built on the island.

The prince was helpless. With genuine belief and trust, he knelt and called up into the sky, "Are there any compassionate beings up there that can protect sentient beings, generating love and compassion?"

He called Tönpa Shenrab's name and said he was building a temple for the benefit of all sentient beings, but he was in danger of not being able to complete the project. He asked if there was anyone who could listen to his inner voice of suffering. He needed their protection and help.

While he was kneeling on the ground and facing towards sky, Sangye Tönpa Shenrab heard him. Immediately, with his entire entourage, he came down to the place where the buildings were being built. He performed the teachings of Nampar Gyalwa, which means "victory over all obstacles." There, he gave the teachings that we still perform when someone dies—when we recite the 100,000 Enlightened Sangye names ceremony (*long gye*).

So, this is just one example of what can happen if we can truly call upon the Enlightened Ones from deep inside with great faith and trust. If we call truly with no doubt, they can protect us.

Taking refuge in the Four Supreme Objects is not like shaking hands with them, person to person. But it is a true inner communication, performed with trust. Trust is the most important; it keeps everything connected. If we have faith and trust in someone, it comforts us, and everything goes smoothly. If we doubt someone, then we cannot take any positive action, because there is always a question that blocks the positive actions in our mind. The doubt needs to be cleared up. True protection only comes when we call and communicate truly—to the Warmhearted Ones, the Lamas, the Enlightened Ones, and the Teachings.

Until we experience the final result, we must continue taking refuge without changing our trust and faith. Then, we will certainly experience the result of that truth. That is how the Sangye helps. The Sangye doesn't come and take our suffering, simply saying, "now you are free." It only happens through the connection with the teachings.

The preliminary part of this teaching is now completed.

IV

Actual Practice

10. Avoiding Non-virtuous Deeds

དང་པོ་སྐྱེས་བུ་ཆུང་བའི་ལམ་སྡུག་བསྔལ་སྡིག་པའི་འབྲས་བུ་རྟོགས་པའི་རྒྱུ་མི་དགེ་བ་ལ་འཛེམ་པ་ནི།

First [actual practice], the path of those with lesser capacity, realizing the result of wrongdoing is suffering, causing the shunning of non-virtue:

ཤིན་ཏུ་མི་བཟོད་ངན་སོང་སྡུག་བསྔལ་ཀུན།

All the suffering of the three lower realms is extremely unbearable

སྡིག་པའི་ལས་ཀྱི་འབྲས་བུ་ཡིན་ཞེས་གསུངས།

And is said to be the result of evil actions.

དེ་ཕྱིར་སྲོག་ལ་བབ་ཀྱང་སྡིག་པའི་ལས།

Therefore, even at the cost of one's life, non-virtuous deeds

ནམ་ཡང་མི་བྱེད་སེམས་ལ་དྲེས་པར་མཛོད།

Are diligently remembered to never be performed.

Now we begin with the "Actual Practice." The first three stanzas of this section start with the three different capacities or levels of understanding on the part of the practitioners. The stanzas state how the capacities of the three different levels are differentiated and determine how each of these types of practitioners should focus their main practice.

ACTUAL PRACTICE

With the path of the lowest level capacity of practitioner, practitioners are called to understand suffering as the consequences of non-virtuous deeds.

Suffering is an unpleasurable sense or feeling—an experience. It is the result of non-virtuous deeds, primarily ignorance. Because of ignorance, the energies of the five poisons all manifest. Because of these five poisons, the non-virtuous deeds—which affect the body, speech, and mind—manifest. These non-virtuous actions will result in unhappiness, sorrow, and misery.

It is important to clearly understand this. Don't just accept it, but in meditation, go into your mind. Look at yourself and see if there is any specific thing that is bothering you. You are likely suffering or unhappy in some way. Go to that specific point you are experiencing and investigate it. Where is it coming from? What circumstances led to it? Is this suffering related to any of the actions of the virtuous deeds? Or is it related to some non-virtuous deeds? Or is it something totally different?

According to the teaching, suffering is all directly connected to non-virtuous deeds, because it connects to our ignorance. We may experience different types of suffering, but the cause is always ignorance. It is like the different colors of a wool blanket—the colors are different, the design is different, the sizes are different, but the quality is always that of wool. Its source is always wool. The wool is the ignorance that manifests all types of poisons. Once you have ignorance, it manifests according to the condition—anger, attachment, jealously, or hatred. The result is unhappiness, misery, and suffering.

The text tells us that our non-virtuous deeds lead us to being born into the three lower realms: the hell realm, hungry ghost realm, and animal realm. These three each have different levels of suffering and misery. We are in the human realm, in the middle, and then there are the demigod and god realms above us. These three are the upper realms. Together, these are the six realms of cyclic existence.

According to the Bön teaching, until you overcome these non-virtuous deeds, you will continue suffering in khorwa (cyclic existence) through the cycles of death and birth and death and birth. The text says, "the unbearable suffering of the lower realms is a result of non-virtuous action." We generally say that anger leads us to be born in the hell realm, ignorance and close-mindedness leads to being reborn in the animal realm, and greed leads us to being born in the hungry ghost realm.

If we don't want to be born in these realms, we must think about the sources of the conditions. We must cut the root or source of the suffering. That way, we automatically prevent ourselves from being reborn in these realms.

In this lowest level of capacity, practitioners realize that the source of all suffering is the result of the non-virtuous deeds and commit to not engage in these in order to protect themselves.

There are ten non-virtuous deeds and ten virtuous deeds. They are divided into three groups: Body, Speech, and Mind.

For the Body category, the non-virtuous deeds are taking a life, stealing something not given to you, and sexual misconduct.

According to the monks' vows, not taking a life means not even the smallest sentient being. But this has three conditions:

the object of the killing, the motive of killing, and the satisfaction of killing. When these three conditions occur, for example, if we feel satisfaction in having killed something, we have broken our vow as a monk. It's about intent and satisfaction. While we are likely to kill tiny bugs as we walk through a park, if we are not intending to do so, and not satisfied at having done so, we have not committed a great non-virtuous deed.

Stealing what is not given or taking anything that does not belong to us is considered a non-virtuous deed.

Sexual misconduct is about physical relationships. For example, it may mean at the wrong time or in the wrong place—like in the temple, or while on retreat, or on special practice days like birthdays of Tönpa Shenrab or Nyammed Sherab Gyaltsen. It also includes having a relationship with someone other than your partner. If you commit adultery, that is sexual misconduct. You could think of it as a moral discipline or as a protection. A lot of problems arise because of sexual relationships. Having relationships with many different people creates problems in society and in friendships. You should be faithful and honest in your relationship. On special days and times, think about remaining in this moral discipline.

The four non-virtuous actions of the Speech category are telling lies, divisive speech, using harsh language, and gossiping.

Telling lies again has different levels depending on whether you are a monk, master, or layperson. If a master goes beyond his abilities and claims to have the capacity to read someone's mind when they don't have that capacity, it is considered telling lies. Or if one pretends to have a vision of a protector who speaks directly to them—these are great lies. This is a negative action toward the teaching. These kinds of lies are very negative and non-virtuous. They are misleading others. They are misleading their belief, faith, and trust in the teaching. When students find that the master is lying, the master's actions may cause them to become discouraged in the Bön Teaching.

Truth has the most powerful quality. Truth may have a bitter taste and be hard to digest, but it lasts forever. We can always rely on it. In day-to-day life, some people are very good at making up stories that are not true. These are also lies. So we should be mindful of what we are saying and control our speech to remain truthful.

Divisive speech is powerfully negative in our daily lives because it causes divisions between people. Friends, families, relationships, and organizations can split because of these words. If somebody has this weakness toward divisive speech, they must work hard to overcome it. Don't say anything that will cause others to separate, suffer, or have anger toward each other. Instead of putting energy into divisive thoughts, try to use words that bring people together. Be mindfully aware as a practitioner. Being a practitioner means to apply things in action. Action related to others' benefit is the action you need to cultivate. This is how we can show that what we are practicing can manifest. Help to solve others' problems and correct their misunderstandings—whatever we can do by speaking to bring people together. This is the opposite of divisive speech.

Think how much negativity you cultivate with divisive speech. If you split up very good friends, think of their suffering

ACTUAL PRACTICE

and unhappiness. They are helpless because of their ignorance and all the negative energy that is going through these two people. By causing this, it becomes your responsibility and your negative karma. You cultivate negative karma this way. Therefore, divisive speech is powerfully negative, and we really must be very careful in our daily lives to avoid it.

And then there is harsh language. This is like a sharp sword cutting someone. We can see a sword and avoid it, but we can't see how words can be a weapon of such sharpness. Words can cut things apart piece by piece, cutting a person's heart inwardly. This is an invisible weapon. Speech can kill another's heart and totally destroy their mental state.

Be careful about using harsh language at all. The more you use harsh language thoughtlessly in your life, the more you become harsh in all your speech. Pay attention to it. Once you are aware of it, you can reduce or overcome this harsh language. Other people will be happier with your language and your expressions. Talk about the good qualities of others, or about things that make people happy and peaceful. Talk about things that people can enjoy. Don't say something unnecessarily harsh, because this hurts people. They may not express it right away, but they are being hurt, and it generates negative karma in you.

The next non-virtuous action of speech is gossiping. Everyone knows about this one. We are very good at this practice. We spend a lot of our time simply gossiping. Gossiping means saying things that have no aim or topic, but we keep talking about all sort of things, whether it's helpful or not helpful. We keep chatting, on and on. In the end, there's no gain or result. Gossiping is just a waste of time. It is diluting and distracting. It keeps us away from our internal quality of wisdom, knowledge, and peaceful qualities.

Telling the truth is the opposite of lying; using words to bring people together is the opposite of divisive speech. Using soft, genuine, honest, gentle language is the opposite of harsh language. Talking meaningfully about things you need to talk about is the opposite of gossip. So, when you have a problem of easily being distracted by gossip, recite some prayers or recitations. This is an easy way to overcome it.

The three non-virtuous deeds in the category of Mind are evil or harmful thoughts toward others, ill will, and wrong view toward the teacher or the teaching.

Harmful thought is based on anger and attachment. It is thinking of something negative, wrong, or harmful—wanting bad things to happen to other people. This is based on jealousy, attachment, and anger. Evil actions all start from the evil thoughts.

Ill will is creating negative thoughts and feelings toward others. It is not valuing or respecting others, having unfriendly or hostile feelings toward them, or directing feelings of dislike, hatred, or resentment toward them. It could be a desire to see others experience harm or discomfort. This is all ill will.

Wrong view toward the teaching means contradicting the view and essence of the teaching, saying there's no rebirth, telling people it's all fake, it's all an illusion, saying there is no law of cause and effect—anything that contradicts the teaching.

ACTUAL PRACTICE

On the positive side, there are three positive, virtuous deeds of the mind: thinking positively of others, facilitating or doing anything that creates a positive result or positive atmosphere, and thinking positively toward others' deeds. We need to trust others. We must have faith and trust in the Bön teaching, even if we don't understand the full essence of it.

The text says to realize the sources of suffering are the negative deeds—the non-virtuous actions. We need to put effort into our own practice so that we do not engage in any negative deeds, because they will lead us to suffer. They will result in negative experiences.

Keeping away from the action and engagement of non-virtuous deeds, we will automatically engage in positive deeds. Participating in any positive deeds, even just being part of something, has great merit. If we are mindful, moment to moment, we are training our mind, so that in every moment we are part of the practice.

11. Searching the Path of Freedom

གཉིས་པ་སྐྱེས་བུ་འབྲིང་གི་ལམ་སྒྲིད་པའི་བདེ་བ་མི་རྟག་པ་རྟོགས་ཤིང་ཐར་པའི་དོན་དུ་གཉེར་བ་ནི།

Second [actual practice], the path of middle level capacity of practitioner, searching the path of liberation by understanding the impermanence of worldly happiness:

འཁོར་བའི་བདེ་བ་རྩྭ་མགོའི་ཟིལ་པ་འད།

Joys of the cyclic world are like dew on the tip of grass.

ཐམས་ཅད་སྐད་ཅིག་མི་རྟག་འགྱུར་བའོ།

All is momentary and impermanent.

ནམ་ཡང་མི་བསླུ་ཐར་པའི་གོ་འཕང་མཆོག

The supreme state of liberation never deceives.

དོན་དུ་གཉེར་བ་རང་སེམས་འདུལ་བར་བྱ།

[Therefore], strive to subdue one's own [untamed] mind.

Everyone talks about wanting freedom, but we each have a different definition of this so-called freedom. We use the same word, but we understand a different meaning. Some think that freedom means they can do anything they like without anyone restraining or disciplining them. Others think of freedom as not being connected to, or dependent on, someone else.

The freedom we talk about here is the total freedom from suffering and its cause—the total freedom to live in a happy environment.

During this material life, in this cyclic existence, joy and comfort is like a water drop on a leaf. It is beautiful, but it is very delicate. The sun can dry the drop of water. Something can touch the drop of water and make it fall off the blade of grass. Dust can dry up the drop of water. It is only momentarily, unstably there. At any moment, it is ready to collapse.

The cyclic condition of existence is temporary. Things exist for a moment, but nothing is permanent. Khorwa keeps us bound with our anger, attachment, hatred, jealously, and ignorance. It binds us tighter and tighter, and the more we are bound, the more we decrease our ability to move freely and with flexibility.

So, we are not free here. We are not free from suffering. We are bound and conditioned by suffering, within an environment of suffering. There is no true freedom of joy or happiness.

The benefits we feel in this life are only temporal. This is not the happiness or comfort we are searching for. Temporal happiness can create a certain level of benefit—a superficial level—but not an ultimate level. This is not to say that material objects have no value or that material goods are not necessary. Material goods provide benefit, because our physical body itself is built up by material conditions. The body needs to be furnished with its material needs. But true freedom is not ultimately dependent on materials. Our practice is meant to overcome material boundaries and give us freedom from material dependency.

Material dependency is limited. Overcome that material dependency and we achieve ultimate freedom—total, everlasting freedom—a freedom we can rely on. It is not created or the result of the conditions of the material world. It is beyond the material condition. This is why we talk about material goods being like the drop of water on the tip of a leaf. These materials are all temporary—we cannot trust them, we cannot rely on them, we can just take advantage of them for the moment that it lasts for our benefit. So, we mustn't be attached to the material, grasp it, or be totally dependent on it. We should learn how to be free from that dependency to discover the ultimate happiness and ultimate freedom.

When we are free from all dependency, what we discover is something we can always rely on. That is the inner wisdom, the inner realization, the inner recognition of our true self—the inner realization of the nature of impermanence. These are all things we need to discover.

To overcome our attachment and grasping, we need to learn how to tame our untamed mind. Again, it goes back to the mind. It is all about using our energy to free ourselves from the boundaries, dependencies, and conditions. Our mind determines our actions, and whether we are collecting the positive or negative karma of our virtuous or non-virtuous deeds.

The text emphasizes transforming the mind in the way we look at and perceive things. Change the way of looking toward the world in a positive direction by focusing the mind. Training the mind simply means training the mind to be focused, looking in the correct and perfect way. If we point our mind in that direction, we can transform our mind; we can transform everything.

If we cannot transform our own mind, then there is no chance we can transform anything else. It is the mind that recognizes the transformation. When our mind is transformed from a negative way of looking to a positive way, and from a wrong view to a positive view, then we will have results. If we can do this perfectly regardless of the situation, we can handle anything. Even the most difficult experience in our lives can be handled easily because we know how to transform it.

12. Generating the Mind of Enlightenment

གསུམ་པ་སྐྱེས་བུ་རབ་ཀྱི་ལམ་སྟོང་ཉིད་སྙིང་རྗེ་ཟུང་འཇུག་ཏུ་བསྒོམ་པ་ནི།

Third [actual practice], as the path of highest level of practitioner, cultivating the unity of emptiness and compassion:

སྲིད་ཞིའི་མཐའ་ལས་གྲོལ་བ་ལ་གསུམ་སྟེ།

To liberate from the extremes of the cyclic world and enlightenment, [there are] three [ways]:

དང་པོ་བྱང་ཆུབ་སེམས་བསྐྱེད་པ་ནི། ༈

First, generating the mind of enlightenment:

ཁམས་གསུམ་སེམས་ཅན་ཕ་མའི་རང་བཞིན་ལ།

Naturally, all beings of three realms of existence [are like our own] parents.

དེ་རྣམས་སྡུག་ན་རང་བདེའི་ཅི་ལ་ཕན།

What is the benefit of one's own pleasure when they are facing hardships?

དེས་ན་མཐའ་ཡས་སེམས་ཅན་སྡུག་བསྔལ་མཚོ།

Endless sentient beings are in an ocean of suffering, therefore,

དེ་ལས་སྒྲོལ་ཕྱིར་བྱང་ཆུབ་སེམས་བསྐྱེད་དོ།

To free them from that [suffering], I generate the mind of enlightenment.

ACTUAL PRACTICE

The main topic here is generating the mind of enlightenment. To generate the mind of enlightenment, on a basic level, we first need the preliminary practices. Then, at a little more advanced level, we must distinguish the non-virtuous and virtuous deeds and understand impermanence—the uncertainty of life and material existence. Then, we go even deeper, with the union of compassion and realization of the true nature of emptiness.

When we talk about emptiness, all the schools of Buddhism and Bön have their own point of view and interpretation of what emptiness is. For example, in Bön, emptiness can be explained according to Dho (Skt. Sutra, the method of which is known as the Path of Renunciation), Ngag (Skt. Tantra, the method of which is known as the Path of Transformation), or Dzogchen (Great Perfection, the method of which is known as the Path of Self-Liberation). These three levels of Bön teaching each have different ways of introducing us to and understanding the nature of emptiness.

No matter which path(s) we follow, we must integrate both compassion and emptiness. To do so, we must understand what these really are. We say, "I generate my mind like the Enlightened Ones." But because we are not enlightened, we are still on the path of practice and training, and we can't generate our minds exactly like the Enlightened Ones. We don't fully understand the philosophy of the mind of enlightenment, what it really means, so we are just grasping the surface level of what enlightenment means—generating good aspirations, good heart, and good will for the benefit of others. This is generally all we understand in the beginning.

The text says, "Naturally, all beings of three realms of existence are like our own parents." All sentient beings have a link to one another. The example here is like the link of parents and children. We are all able to understand the concept of the connection of parents and children, raised with kindness and love. Our parents have sacrificed for our benefit. They sacrificed themselves to give us comfort and make us happy. This example helps us understand the concept of compassion.

Because others have been kind toward us, we now have the responsibility to show kindness to others. Therefore, we practice to reach enlightenment so that we will have the full capacity to liberate and free others from this cycle of suffering. We can't do this while we are in the same state of suffering. Only those manifested Enlightened Ones like Gyalwa Nyipa, "The Second Lord," Nyammed Sherab Gyaltsen, or other great masters, who manifested as human beings on purpose in order to liberate sentient beings can do this. In general, all sentient beings are born in the same form, out of the force of our karma and our ignorance. It is not our own choice. Instead, it is our negative karma and ignorance that keeps bringing us back.

We need to understand and develop the mind of enlightenment to reach enlightenment. Without generating the mind of enlightenment, we are not able to enter even the first stage of the path of training. There are four paths of training to achieve enlightenment. The fifth is the resultant path, beyond the training. The four paths are gradual steps. The first stage of the training path begins the moment one generates the mind of enlightenment (*Jang Chub Sem*). Without entering the path of training, we will not be able to enter the second, third, fourth, or resultant paths. So, it is essential to enter this path by generating the mind of enlightenment.

In plain words, learn how to dedicate yourself totally for the benefit of other beings. Dedicate yourself truly and genuinely, your whole life, as much as you can, to benefit others. Do anything that causes joy, benefit, or peace for others. This doesn't mean you must become a monk or nun—just do whatever you can that causes others happiness. By doing this, you are entering into the path of enlightenment. Bit by bit, you need to develop this.

If an action is good, but the motive is wrong, it is not a positive action—like giving poisoned food to a mouse. Here, the action is giving, but the motive is to kill. So, it is not a virtuous deed. We must look at our motive for doing things. To do so, train the mind. It always comes down to mind. Transforming our entire way of thinking seems difficult—like becoming a totally new person—but it is not exactly like that. Our inner mind is like a wild horse tied up with rope. The horse can only go as far as the rope allows. In the beginning, we must train the mind like we would train a wild horse, by applying a mindful practice the way we would keep the horse on a rope. Then, after a certain time, we don't need the rope. Our mind adapts as well, and we no longer need any force to control it. Here, in this practice, we are training our mind to make ourselves warm-hearted toward others.

There are two types of "mind of enlightenment"—relative mind of enlightenment (*Kunzob Sem Kyed*) and absolute mind of enlightenment (*Dhondam Sem Kyed*).

The relative mind of enlightenment inclues both Aspiration Semkyed and Action Semkyed. The absolute mind of enlightenment is based on the realization of the true natural state of mind, and within that, also taking any action for the sake of all beings with compassion.

The relative mind of enlightenment is meant to generate positive good will toward all others—to have compassionate wishes for their freedom from suffering. It is thinking what we can do to facilitate or cause good things for others.

There is a small difference between compassion and our mind of enlightenment thought. Both are thoughts. Compassion is the wish for all sentient beings to be free from suffering. It's a prayer of aspiration, wanting all sentient beings to be free from suffering and the cause of suffering—wanting all sentient beings to be happy and perfected. This is the concept of compassion.

The mind of enlightenment is slightly different. When we say we want to free all beings from suffering, we are also saying that we wish to take action to actually help free others from their suffering. It's more than just wishing for all beings to be free of suffering. It is the concept of actions we can take to make that happen. Having this always in our mind is the way we develop it. It will grow in meditation. It will grow in action if we apply it. We may not immediately change, but this is the beginning.

ACTUAL PRACTICE

As an example, in India, the buses are always very crowded. If there is an elderly person or someone who needs help, we can stand up and give them our seat. By giving them the seat, we are not liberating them, but by giving temporary comfort, it sows the seed of discovering ultimate comfort. By giving them a little comfort, we are training our own mind how to put the practice in action. Little by little, it affects our daily life.

Any way we can condition ourselves to make small sacrifices for others is developing the relative and ultimate mind of enlightenment. It is conditioning us. By putting this in practice over and over, it grows in us, and it becomes part of our being. It soon becomes more natural to think about what we can do to help others.

According to the capacity of the individual, the mind of enlightenment can be divided into three levels or examples. The first level of the mind of enlightenment is like a shepherd, watching over the flock. The second is like a tour guide, trying to visit places first, before leading a tour. The third is like a ferry boat captain who keeps everyone together and gets them to the other side of the river safely, and at the same time. These three are all engaged in doing something for others but with slightly different views.

The shepherd thinks of the animals first—about where to find good grass, water, or safety from wild animals. When the shepherd knows the area is safe, they allow the animals to roam there. This is one example of the mind of enlightenment.

The second one is like a tour guide who practices in order to gain enlightenment first and then lead all sentient beings to enlightenment. To liberate all other sentient beings, we must generate enlightenment for ourselves first, but gaining enlightenment should not be our true motive. We only want it so we can provide enlightenment for others. We should still be thinking about others first.

The third level is wanting something for others, but wanting that for yourself as well, at the same time. The ferryman will ferry others to get to the destination (like enlightenment) and they will all get there at the same time. The ferryman is not specifically focusing on other sentient beings. They are thinking that if they benefit, others benefit, and if others benefit, they benefit. It is for both.

The text of *Dzod Kun Tu* gives these three examples. We must think of our own capacity in this regard. Are we the shepherd who thinks of the animals first? Are we the tour guide who checks out a location before leading others? Or are we the ferry boat captain, who takes everyone across together? If we can, try to think like shepherds. Think of all sentient beings first. Desire that they be safe and secure and have everything they need. Focus on their benefit, not thinking about your own comfort. Dedicating yourself in action makes this possible. The true mind of enlightenment is about taking action, even sacrificing ourselves for others if we must.

In an earlier lifetime, Sangye Tönpa Shenrab sacrificed his own life to protect other beings. One time, when he was in the hell realm, he and another person were pulling a horse cart. The two of them were pulling one cart, but it was too heavy for them. So, Sangye Tönpa Shenrab generated the mind of enlightenment and thought that even though they were both suffering and unable to pull the cart, maybe he could try to pull the cart by himself and let the other person have a rest. After generating this concept, he asked the hell realm guardians to let the other person rest. All the hell realm guards yelled wildly saying, "Who do you think you are, to think of others? Everyone here is meant to be purified of their own karmic deeds. You each must pay for your own karmic deeds, so mind your own business." And he hit a hammer on the Sangye's head, causing the death of Tönpa Shenrab right there.

We can think of this story in two different ways. First, we can think that he died for nothing. If he'd stayed quiet and continued to pull the cart, he would not have died. But if we look at it from the positive side, he was freed from the suffering of the hell realm, because of his practice of genuine concern for the other person. If he had not had that concept of compassion and good will toward his friend and tried to pull the cart himself, he may not have died. He died because the power of his compassion and his true mind of enlightenment made him free from that suffering of the hell realm. That is the power of the practice.

Again, in another of Tönpa Shenrab's past lives, there were three brothers. During a time of famine, they sacrificed their wealth to feed the poor people. They even sacrificed their own bodies to feed the starving people. In the end, they were free from cyclic existence and achieved the ultimate state of enlightenment. But this was only because they had such a powerful practice. On the material level, it seems like they are being foolish, dying for others. But if we look at it in a positive way, they simply transformed their material body into a body of enlightenment.

The mention above of the two Semkyeds is what we mean when we talk about the mind of enlightenment. Build it up little by little through practice. For example, meditate on another person's suffering. Try to experience the sense of that suffering—how it is bothering and hurting them. Think about how healthy, joyful, and lucky you are in your own conditions. Think how good they would feel if they had your same sense of joy and comfort. Then mentally, in meditation, transform that. Take their pain and suffering out of their body and put your joy and happiness into their body. Try to experience their happiness. If you can contemplate on that, you are taking an action, at least on the level of meditation. This alone has a certain quality that can benefit them.

To generate the true mind of enlightenment, having true compassion is most important.

For another practice, you should:

1. Think of all sentient beings as having once been your mother.
2. Think of their kindness to you when they were your mother.
3. When you remember their kindness, think of wanting to repay their kindness when they need it.
4. Think of generating joy and happiness for them. Be kind, genuine, and gentle to them.

From this practice of compassion in meditation comes genuine, true compassion. True compassion means unconditional compassion. Everyone has compassion. Even the wildest animals have compassion. They will kill to feed their own children, which is out of their love and compassion. The compassion we are talking about here is unconditional compassion. Don't think about yourself only in selfish way. Think about this other being as your own mother or your child.

When you have truly practiced and generated compassion and the mind of enlightenment, when difficult circumstances arise and there is a need for action, you will have no doubt and no fear. You will not be afraid of catching someone else's sickness. If you have a true mind of enlightenment, you don't have any limits or boundaries, you just perform the action that is needed. Even if you get sick, you will accept it, because you are doing it for others completely selflessly.

Compassion has the power to heal. It has the power to transform. Compassion has the power to create unity and a peaceful environment. Quietly meditating on compassion can provide a total cure.

13. Exchanging Your Happiness with One Who is Suffering

གཉིས་པ་སྦྱོར་བ་བྱང་ཆུབ་སེམས་དཔའི་སྒོམ་པ་ལ་གཉིས་ཏེ།

Second [way to liberate from the extremes of the cyclic world and enlightenment], meditation on enlightened mind has two types:

༈ དང་པོ་ཀུན་རྫོབ་བྱང་ཆུབ་སེམས་ལ་གཉིས་ལས།

First, the two activities of the relative mind of enlightenment:

དང་པོ་མཉམ་བཞག་རང་གཞན་རྗེ་བ་ནི།

[Of these], first, the meditative contemplation of exchanging oneself with others:

སྡུག་བསྔལ་མ་ལུས་རང་བདེ་འདོད་ལས་བྱུང་།

The source of all suffering is selfishly desiring happiness for oneself.

རྫོགས་པའི་སངས་རྒྱས་གཞན་ཕན་སེམས་ལས་འབྱུང་།

The accomplishment of perfect enlightenment comes from considering the welfare of others.

དེ་ཕྱིར་བདག་བདེ་གཞན་གྱི་སྡུག་བསྔལ་གཉིས།

Therefore, my happiness, and the suffering of others,

ཡང་དག་བརྗེ་བར་སེམས་ཀྱི་ངེས་པར་ནུས།

[I] am truly able to exchange [these] with the power of mind.

We do not wish to go through suffering, but we go through suffering because of the forces of our own karma. Other sentient beings also have no wish to suffer, but they are also going through their own karma. Like all beings, we want joy and comfort, but suffering is caused by our negative karma.

The text describes exchanging one's happiness with another's suffering. This is a practice for the sake of others. Wanting them to have happiness, we totally dedicate ourselves to developing the power of thought to put ourselves in the other's place as they are suffering.

We are trying to make an exchange with them, giving suffering people our own pleasure and joy. This is the kind of training we need—training to think this way regularly. Gradually, we develop the ability to easily sacrifice minor things for others' benefit.

Think of the other person and exchange your happiness with their suffering. Practice in this way as much as you can. Then, consider your actions. Think how much energy, time, and money you spend to help others. Think about what you are doing to help others through volunteering, giving charity, helping someone elderly clean their house, and so on.

In the beginning, we may want to help people that we know, and we learn to enjoy doing that. But the aim of our practice is not only to help those we know, but everyone, without conditions, just for the joy of it. It is not enough to just help others; we need to enjoy doing it. Generate the joy of doing something for others. Then, that action has a quality. Anyone can do something to help, but enjoying what we are doing to relieve others' suffering is very powerful. In time, it will be part of our nature.

Don't expect others' gratitude or appreciation in return. If we do this, our practice isn't really for others. True compassion is free of expectations. The more we realize happiness because of what we are doing, the more it will encourage us to continue. And then, each and every moment that we must do something for others, we won't hesitate. We will happily be ready to do it.

As for the concept of exchanging, think of someone else's suffering or think of your suffering. When you have suffered, was it pleasurable? No. Suffering is difficult; it is sad; it is unhappy; it is sorrowful. Think, "As I have been through this same misery, so I would like to do anything I can to make other people comfortable. I'm glad that I can help other people. I'm happy that I have this opportunity."

We can think of the suffering of others as being a great teacher because it allows us to practice. It gives us an opportunity to put our practice into action. When there is no violence, there is little chance for compassion. When there is no hopelessness, there is little chance to practice compassion. The Enlightened Ones do not need our compassion. They do not need our help. We, the sentient beings, need help because we are not ready to take care of ourselves.

When you practice, don't force it at the very beginning. Just do what makes you feel comfortable. This will allow you to expand your capacity for being spontaneous.

We need to do this spontaneously rather than forcefully. We might start with force and effort, but we try to reach the stage of spontaneous compassion. This way, we will spontaneously be of service for other beings, easily taking any action that is needed.

In the early days, the great practitioners practiced this love and compassion for others. If there was someone with no clothing, the great masters would simply give them their clothes. If you think that you want to do this, but you're afraid you're going to feel cold, then you are not truly practicing exchanging yourself for others. You have not developed the capacity for truly sacrificing yourself for others' needs and their happiness.

Even if we have very little and only have a small amount to share, still share. Even giving another person the very little you have can generate true happiness and joy in them. We are not freeing them from khorwa, but we are creating true joy and appreciation in them. That is how we cultivate the practice.

Always have the motive of helping others, even if you don't feel you have enough for yourself. You can still practice through your motivation of compassion and enlightened mind.

When we talk about exchanging—taking someone's suffering and giving them our joy—we can do this practice in meditation. Visualize anyone you think of who is suffering. If the person is in front of you, that is good, but if not, you can just visualize how the person is suffering. Focus on that suffering and try to experience that sense of suffering.

Inhale and hold the breath at the level of your navel. While you are inhaling, think that you are removing all that person's sickness or suffering. You are taking it out of their body. Think that you have taken out all their suffering with that breath, and you are bringing it into yourself and hold it in your navel.

As you exhale, put all your energy and joy and happiness into them. When you breathe out with total joy and happiness, feel that the other person now has your joy and your freedom from suffering. If you practice this often, you may physically have the experience of goose bumps, or you may cry or have another spontaneous reaction. Doing this often gives you the strength and quality of the true mind of enlightenment. It gives true compassion and joy.

You may wonder if by taking the other person's suffering, you will suffer. The answer is both yes and no. It depends on your level of practice. If you are only taking away their suffering and putting it into yourself, you may get some symptoms or signs that something is happening to you. It will not make you sick, and it will only happen sometimes. You are not objectively bringing the sickness into you. But through the visualization, you are bringing the karmic negative energy into you through your breath. When you bring it into your body, you should integrate it into the nature of emptiness, into the nature of spaciousness, into open space.

When you throw a sword up into space it never cuts or does damage to the space. It does not leave an imprint in space. Similarly, if you can integrate that negative quality into the nature of spaciousness—the nature of its own true, open space of emptiness—then you will not suffer. You simply integrated that energy into the space of emptiness. The person suffers because they don't have enough capacity to integrate their suffering into the wisdom of the Nature of Mind. So, practice that way. It is tremendously helpful.

It can also be helpful if the person who is suffering is with you, and you are practicing as a group. You all inhale that suffering and hold it in, imagining that all the sickness and suffering from that person comes out of that person's body and enters you as you breathe in. And then you hold it. As you hold the breath, you are contemplating on the suffering's true nature of its spaciousness.

When you breathe out, visualize transmitting all the joy and happiness into that person. That person receives your sense of joy and peace. See the person as healthy, happy, and healed. Remain in that state until you feel that that person is completely healed and recovered.

If there is a specific person you think needs healing, do this practice regularly. That doesn't mean they have to be physically ill, but they can be going through financial problems or relationship problems. They may not know what decision to make to overcome their problems. Whatever the problem, think of it. Take that problem into yourself and integrate it into spaciousness. Send the energy of your friendship and love to them. Feel that the person is being filled with joy and happiness. Feel they have the power to overcome their challenges.

Tong means relieving, *Len* means taking. *Tong Len* is what we are practicing. You are relieving and taking the suffering of others. You are taking it into yourself, and you are giving them the generosity of your own comfort and joy. This will not reduce your comfort; you will increase your comfort and joy because you have increased your capacity for joy.

There was a great Dzogchen master who was traveling from one place to another. He saw a woman who was in great pain, suffering and shouting. By just passing near her and noticing her pain, it awakened in him a great compassion for her, and he practiced *Tong Len*. Immediately, the woman was relieved of her pain and suffering because the master took the pain. It was temporarily painful for him, but he knew how to integrate and transform it. He didn't hold onto that pain because he was able to transform it. Similarly, don't feel that you are going to suffer by doing this; just be free to do what you need to do in any moment. This is the real mind of enlightenment.

14. Bringing Robbery onto the Path

གཉིས་པ་རྗེས་ཐོབ་ལམ་འཁྱེར་ལ་བཅུ།

Second [activity of the relative mind of enlightenment], bringing post-meditation [experiences you are encountering] onto the path, [of which there are] ten [parts]:

ཞུད་པོ་འཕྲོག་བཅོམ་ལམ་བྱེར་ནི།

First, bringing robbery onto the path:

སུ་དག་འདོད་ཆེའི་བདག་གི་ཟས་ནོར་ཀུན།

Whoever may have greatly desired all my food and wealth,

ཐམས་ཅད་འཕྲོག་ནས་ཁྱེར་དུ་སོང་ན་ཡང་།

Even though they rob me and carry everything away,

མ་ཡིས་བུ་བཞིན་སྐྱོང་བའི་སེམས་བསྐྱེད་ནས།

Like a mother cares for her own child, I generate the mind of enlightenment [toward them].

དུས་གསུམ་དགེ་བ་གང་བགྱིས་དེ་ལ་བསྔོ།

I dedicate all merits for them, whatever virtuous deeds cultivated in the Three Times.

What is the best way to apply practice if you have been robbed or have lost something? The answer is very simple and clear.

When people are robbed, they are often very unhappy, disappointed, or have a very negative reaction. People never have a positive reaction to being robbed. But it says here that this is the wrong way to think.

Whatever we've lost or had stolen, it is gone from us. The only thing to do is to use this as part of our practice and make it positive. The masters are guiding us here to put this experience into practice. Materially, we may have lost something, but spiritually, we have gained a lot. That gain is far more important than what we have lost materially.

Think that what you have lost was needed more by the person who stole it from you and be glad that your belongings could benefit them. Dedicate your belongings to them and let them go. At least this way you are generating good merit and not cultivating more negative karma.

Look at enemies positively because they give you an opportunity to practice. Transform your tragedies into practice. Pray that the thief will change and transform their heart, so they won't collect any more bad karma. Have compassion for them. You can buy material possessions, but spiritual gains cannot be bought. You can cultivate them only by your own effort, applying yourself in practice.

One time, there was a master living in a hermitage. He was very famous and had lots of visitors who made offerings to him. The robbers of that area thought he might have a lot of things they could steal. In the night, they went to that master and found an empty cave. The master only had tsampa to eat. He told them that they were welcome to have the tsampa, but that they would not find anything else, because he never saw anything else during the day, so they would not find anything there at night.

Instead of acting negatively toward them or saying harsh words, he simply shared everything he had. That sense of love, peacefulness, and compassion made them ashamed. They came the next day and brought offerings and prostrated to the master, and they became practitioners. It gave the master the opportunity to practice and led the robbers to a dharmic life.

In the same way, if you lose something you must learn not to get angry. When you first notice that you have lost something, just pray that it will benefit someone else. That way, it becomes an offering, a practice of generosity. Holding onto it is attachment; being angry or using harsh words is practicing non-virtuous deeds. We must be aware when these moments for practice arise and know how to practice. Our daily life should be lived with the awareness of this opportunity for practice.

15. Bringing Annihilation onto the Path

གཉིས་པ་ཆར་བཅད་ལམ་བྱེར་ནི།

Second, bringing annihilation onto the path:

བདག་ལ་ཉེས་པ་ཅུང་ཟད་མེད་པ་ལ།

Without even the smallest fault on me,

དབང་ཆེན་ཡུས་སྒོག་མགོ་བོ་བཅད་ན་ཡང་།

Even if one is cutting off my head or taking my life,

སྙིང་རྗེས་ཁོ་ཡིས་སྡིག་པ་ངས་ལེན་ཞིང་།

With compassion, I take his evil deeds on to me.

སླར་ཡང་བདག་གིས་བྱང་ལམ་འདྲེན་པར་འགྱུར།

Moreover, I will lead him to the path of enlightenment.

This is very hard to practice, but it is not impossible. We must build up our readiness inside. For now, we are talking about going into the energy in our bodies—going into our heart channel and building up our strength to transform our thinking in this way. But someday, some people will need to put this into practice in their outer lives.

The text says that even if someone is threatening our life, try not to react in a negative way—with anger, hatred, or jealousy. Instead, generate love and compassion. Pray for them. Pray that the person will transform. Pray to the protectors or the deities.

When you are not able to have that kind of thought, if it is something you cannot do, at least think of Sidpe Gyalmo, Chamma, Khyung Mar, etc.—a practice you have familiarity with. Ask the deity for strength and power to not react. Ask for the strength to let you transform the experience.

People often say that if someone is mean to us, we must be strong and fight back; we cannot show that we are weak. But this only trains our egos. As practitioners, we train children to run away rather than fight back. In other traditions, children are taught to fight. Instead, we must train to fight the ego and to run away from the poisons. It is very difficult.

During the Cultural Revolution, many great practitioners were tortured. Some had a very violent reaction. But some, no matter how much they were beaten, maintained a positive mind. Those were the great practitioners that had the power to transform.

Khadro Dechen Wangmo was an extraordinary woman. She was known as a reincarnation of one of the consorts of the great Tertön (Rediscoverer Master) of the Kham region. She passed away in 1987. When they tortured her, everyone thought she would die. Even though she was out in the cold winter, steam would rise from her body. She kept saying that she had compassion for the torturers and asked the deities for their help. She had such great ability that she did not suffer. Compassion gave her the energy inside to not suffer.

Even if something is not life threatening but someone is still acting evil toward you, don't react with anger. Think gently toward them. Let them do whatever they want without reaction.

Just observing it this way gives you a strength of patience and love. And that silent observation has the potential to ease and soften the anger of the other person toward you.

There is a very good Indian movie that the teachers recommend to the children. It is a modernized Hindi movie based on Mahatma Gandhi's philosophy. In the movie, there is a man living on the third floor of an apartment building. When he is leaving to go to work, he spits on the side of a door of a person on the second floor.

The person on the second floor asked what he should do, and he was told, "Every morning, go out and smile at him, and when he spits, just clean it up. And just keep cleaning it every day."

After just a few days of this, the man stopped spitting and apologized. That is how powerful quiet nonreaction can be. You can simply say or show, "Thank you for allowing me to practice." By just observing your reactions, it has the power to transform the person or situation. You are transforming the other person's thoughts. The more someone is trying to be harmful to you, try to be good to them. Speak to them nicely. Offer to help them. Do something positive, and in the end, love, compassion, and nonviolence will always win, because that is the truth of the teaching. Otherwise, what is the use of the practice? Why should a practitioner always have to suffer, if it were possible for suffering to provide the result of joy and happiness?

So, first practice to not react, just to observe. Then practice responding positively and nonviolently. Then practice appreciating the harmful person as a great teacher that shows you how to strengthen your practice.

16. Taking Gossip as the Path

གསུམ་པ་མི་སྙན་སྒྲོག་པའི་ལམ་བྱེར་ནི།

Third, the way to put unfavored gossip [about oneself] onto the path:

འགའ་ཞིག་བདག་ལ་མི་སྙན་སྣ་ཚོགས་པས།

Someone [says] many unpleasant things about me,

འཇིག་རྟེན་ཁྱབ་པར་རྒྱན་དུ་སྒྲོགས་ན་ཡང་།

Even proclaiming it continuously everywhere.

བརྩེ་བའི་སེམས་ཀྱི་སླར་ཡང་དེ་དག་གི

But with love and kindness to them,

ཡོན་ཏན་ཡིན་པ་བདག་གི་དག་ལ་བརྗོད།

I will praise [them] and talk about their good qualities.

Here is another stanza talking about applying the practice in our daily life. It talks about how we should react to gossip.

If someone gossips or talks badly about us, we don't have to do the same against them. That should not be our goal. Instead, we should always look at their qualities.

People make mistakes; that is part of our weakness as a human being. If someone does something to us that we don't like, what makes us different as a practitioner?

If we are fully aware that we are not at fault and that we have not committed any wrongs, then we don't have to worry about what other people say. We don't need to waste our time with it.

Simply be quiet. We don't need to try to clarify the things they are saying about us. It may be best to just pretend we didn't hear it. That way, we learn how to be quiet and patient.

We will know not to retaliate, because we know how unhappy these actions will make us. Wish that the other person will change their attitude and stop saying bad things about other people. Just being silent and observing has an energy and quality. If we can stay quiet, other people will see the truth and will ultimately have more respect for us. As long as we are not guilty or wrong, we don't have to worry about what other people say.

What we are doing is the true basis of the practice. We can't run after each and every person to clarify what has been said about us. It's best to just stay quiet and calm.

Gossiping has no aim, power, or strength of truth. It is just gossip. Some people are very good at it and enjoy it. Let them be that way and only speak of their positive qualities.

17. Taking Criticism as the Path

བཞི་པ་སྐྱོན་འདོགས་ལམ་བྱེར་ནི།

Fourth, the way to put criticism [about oneself] onto the path:

འགྲོ་མང་འཚོགས་པའི་དབུས་སུ་ཁ་གཅིག་གིས།

If someone, in the middle of a public assembly,

སྐྱོན་མེད་སྐྱོན་འདྲུག་ཚིག་རྩུབ་སྨྲས་ན་ཡང་།

Falsely criticizes or uses harsh words [about me],

དེ་ལ་དགེ་བཤེས་ཡིན་པའི་འདུ་ཤེས་ཀྱི།

I will remember that I'm a practitioner,

གུས་པས་འདུན་པ་དགའ་སེམས་བདག་ལ་ཡོད།

And I'll have respect and wish joy for them.

If you are thinking or doing good for others, do it honestly and genuinely. Though, even if you are always honest and genuine, at some point, there will always be someone who does not appreciate or understand, and who will disrespect you. This is normal.

We are not all enlightened. Everyone has a different personality and energy. People act differently. If someone is critical of us, it doesn't mean we need to change our way of living or way of thinking—as long as we are being true.

If we are not true, whatever is being criticized, we must work to change. We don't have to criticize them in return; it will not solve the problem.

We must follow our own path of practice based on the teachings. We do this honestly and genuinely according to the truth. If we commit an honest mistake due to misunderstanding, we should understand and accept this.

There will always be disagreements and people criticizing us. This just proves we all have a different level of understanding different things. If we were all at the same level of understanding, there would not be any need for discussion. But this is not possible. The important thing is that we are pure and genuine.

Often, the Enlightened One, Tönpa Shenrab, was criticized. But he never stood up and ran after everyone who criticized him, trying to correct them. He just did what he needed to do and wished that people would think the right way. In the end, everybody understood and realized the truth.

If someone says you are bad, you know you are not necessarily bad. If someone says you are good, you are also not necessarily good. You are only good in that person's eyes for certain reasons. You could be bad in the eyes of someone else.

What are you really? Think about this.

Criticism is just an action of thought. If ten people criticize you and ten people praise you, which are you more deserving of? Can you divide your body up into those parts?

Don't run after criticism. Don't disturb your inner stability, peacefulness, and calm. Rather, think of it as your practice. Criticism is good to help you progress inwardly. If someone criticizes you, take the opportunity for inner reflection. This gives you the chance to see for yourself who you really are. Are you as good (or bad) as you thought?

ACTUAL PRACTICE

Think of others' criticism of you as a mirror—not one that necessarily shows something negative, but one that allows you to reflect on who or what you really are.

18. Apply Practice to Mistreatment by One's Own Family

ལྔ་པ་གནོད་བྱེད་བརྙས་པ་ལམ་བྱེད་ནི།

Fifth, the way to put scorn from family members onto the path:

བདག་གི་ཕ་མ་བུ་བཞིན་བྱམས་པའི་མིས།

The people whom I care for as my own parents and children,

བདག་ལ་རྟག་ཏུ་དགྲ་རུ་བྱེད་ན་ཡང་།

Even though they always treat me as an enemy,

ནད་ཀྱིས་བཏབས་པའི་བུ་ལ་མ་བཞིན་དུ།

Like a sick child is cared for by their mother,

ལྷག་པར་བརྩེ་བའི་བྱམས་སེམས་བདག་ལ་ཡོད།

I still care for them with love and compassion.

This is another practical stanza. We may have been abused by our families or parents. This text says that we should transform this abuse and apply it in our practice—not in a negative way but rather transform it into a positive practice of love and compassion.

There are always people that we will consider part of our own family—whether they are truly family, or they are friends we've made throughout our life. And despite helping them in life, sometimes these same people, in return, treat us badly or abuse us. This can make us feel broken. We think we could bear it if some stranger did these things to us, but it's much harder if it comes from a close friend or family member.

When we have the realization of the abuse, there is a moment that is energized. We may want to transform ourselves in a negative way and become mean or vengeful toward them. We may want to do the same negative action to them that they have done to us. How does this make us any different from them? We cannot gain anything this way; we can only lose.

Perhaps in this instance, we have lost the freedom of joy, calmness, and flexibility. Our peacefulness is totally destroyed. We spend every moment carrying the problem with us, as if it were a fresh wound. By doing this, we cultivate negative karma, which gives us a result of even more unhappiness.

Instead, the text is telling us we should generate love, compassion, and support for them—despite how difficult this may seem. This is the time to apply the practice. Often, we lose control and take on the same energy level as the person who is angry, and we argue. But this is the time to apply the practice. If nothing else, sit quietly, calm down, and talk.

Arguing does not solve problems. The text says that when someone in your family mistreats you, just generate compassion. Practice patience. It is not easy, but as a practitioner, you don't want to respond the same way that others respond. If you simply hold and refuse to get angry, the other person will stop. The level of energy will calm down, and it will give the situation a chance to come to understanding.

Whenever there is an opportunity, realize it as the time to apply the practice.

19. How to Treat Outsiders Who Mistreat You

དྲུག་པ་ཕྱི་མིས་བཀྲས་པ་ལམ་བྱེར་ནི།

Sixth, the way to put scorn from outsiders onto the path:

རང་དང་མཉམ་པའི་སྐྱེ་བོ་ཁ་གཅིག་གིས།

Even if someone who is my equal [in a situation],

ང་རྒྱལ་དབང་གིས་བཀྲས་ཐབས་བྱེད་ན་ཡང་།

Bullies me with their pride and tries to subjugate me,

བླ་མ་བཞིན་དུ་གུས་པས་བདག་ཉིད་ཀྱི།

I will respectfully, like a Lama,

སྤྱི་བོར་ལེན་པའི་རང་སེམས་བདག་ལ་ཡོད།

Honor and treat them with humility.

This stanza now discusses someone who you don't know, or someone who is your equal or peer. If they insult or denigrate you, or they treat you like you don't know anything, you can just let them do so. It doesn't mean they are right, but by staying calm and humble, it shows that you understand what's important in the situation.

There is something to be gained in this situation because you can practice. You should not expect to gain anything by arguing with them, so let them win. You don't actually lose anything when they win, and you build the strength of your practice. Don't feel shame or feel bad about not replying, especially in public. Being calm when others are mistreating you shows you to be stronger than what some others may think.

Everyone deserves love and respect. Why are we so ignorant and disregarding of that quality? If we are mistreated, we are not happy. So, why do we treat other people like that, thinking they will not mind?

In the movie Seven Years in Tibet, there is a scene I do not like. Two Tibetan leaders are coming down the hill on horses and their assistants have no horses. The assistants are running with the horses but have no horses themselves. This is what happens when we do not have the trained mind of a practitioner. Respect everyone and treat everyone equally as a human being.

Everyone has the same potential of mind. Respect that and don't abuse anyone. Don't disrespect anyone. Don't generate hate; generate compassion and love. We must transform negative situations to positive ones in this way.

20. How to Apply Poverty and Downfall in the Path

བདུན་པ་རྒུད་པ་ལམ་བྱེར་ནི།

Seventh, the way to put downfall onto the path:

ཟས་ནོར་ལོངས་སྤྱོད་མ་ལུས་ཀུན་ཟད་ཅིང་།

Even if all my food, wealth, and possessions are used up,

ལུས་ལ་ནད་བཏབ་ཉལ་ས་ནང་དུ་ལུས།

And my body is ill, lying in bed,

གཞན་བདེ་རང་སྡུག་འདི་ནི་སུས་མ་ལན།

Who is to blame for others' happiness or my own suffering?

སྔོན་ལས་ཡིན་པས་སྡུག་བསྔལ་ང་ལ་མེད།

Since it is due to previous karma, I feel no suffering.

People are often being disrespected or disregarded because they are poor. If we are poor, we have a lot of worries, concerns, and sadness. But we shouldn't be jealous of what other people have. We should be satisfied with ourselves the way we are.

Whatever state we are in is due to our own karma—cause and effect. We should accept this, understand it, and be satisfied with it. We should not be concerned with what other people have and what we might not have.

Don't compare yourself to others. If you do look around, you will also see that you are not the poorest person. You are lucky to have something that others don't have, even your own life, which should give you a reason to feel satisfied. You must be satisfied with what you have. This gives you a space that allows you to move within the nature of perfection.

Do practices that cultivate merit. Do purification practices or mandala practices to purify your karma. When you purify your karma of the negativities, practice cultivating merit or generosity. These actions will give you the results of perfection.

This is how you should look at the situation, rather than thinking that you are poor. Even multimillionaires are not satisfied and happy. Material goods are not the source of happiness. Happiness is something you must generate within your own self. Material prosperity has power and is important, but it is not the true source of happiness and power.

21. Understanding How to Be Satisfied

བརྒྱད་པ་འབྱོར་བའི་ལམ་བྱེད་ནི།

Eighth, the way to put wealth onto the path:

སྙན་གྲགས་སྟོང་གསུམ་ཁྱབ་ཅིང་འགྲོ་མང་གུས།

My fame spreads over the three thousand worlds, and people respect me.

རྣམ་ཐོས་བུ་ཡི་ནོར་འདྲ་འབྱོར་ལྡན་ཅིང་།

My wealth is like a treasury of a wealth deity.

སྲིད་ནོར་སྙིང་པོ་མེད་པར་མ་ཤེས་ན།

If I don't realize the essence-less of worldly wealth,

སེམས་སྟོང་ཁོངས་བྱེད་མེད་པ་བདག་གིས་མཐོང་།

I see nothing can fill my empty mind.

Often, people get too caught up in the material world and always want more and more wealth or fame, even if they are in a well-off situation. Often such people do not think of sharing what they have. Unfortunately, these people do not realize that the unsatisfied mind never has a limit of enough, and at the end, that wealth and its trappings can be gone in a flash. All they have left is a mind of dissatisfaction.

We may be respected or well-known. We may have a high position, great wealth, or a good reputation. If we don't realize that we are fortunate, we will not feel that we have everything that we need. Our need will not end; it will continue to increase. The space of our relative, conventional mind is like an empty sky. It has no limit or end. Empty space never fills up. Empty mind can only fill up when our empty Nature of Mind says it is full. Otherwise, empty space can create more empty space, and we will continue running after trying to fill it, never being able to ground ourselves.

Practice needs to be applied in day-to-day life. When you have good fortune because of your karmic merit or because of your talent or skill, you feel rich. You may have money; you may have relationships and happiness, etc., but there is no guarantee that you will have these forever. They may be momentary. So, make what you have meaningful and apply it in a positive way.

You can use your material wealth to support your practice. You can balance the wealth and spirituality. If your wealth is hindering your spirituality, then your wealth has no value. Material wealth needs to be used at the right time. The advantage of having this is that you can do good deeds for the benefit of other sentient beings. You can cultivate merit by sponsoring, helping others, etc. Then this supports your spiritual development, and your wealth is meaningful. If you don't use it properly, tomorrow may be too late. Act now for others, being skillful by taking the right actions.

In Tibet, we don't have a lot of opportunity to donate, but we give spiritually by sponsoring prayers, sponsoring the construction of stupas and temples, etc. But nowadays, we don't need to do everything on a religious basis. Look at the people who are suffering in Africa and other places. People are being victimized. If you are comfortable, try to help even one other human being. Helping one person to become a good human being is more important than spending your whole life in retreat, because you are transforming one person's total life.

In the end, what is the aim of our practice? We say we practice in order to achieve enlightenment, but why do we want enlightenment? Because we think we can do more for other peoples' benefit.

But what does it mean to be of benefit for other sentient beings? Solving other people's problems is the practical meaning. Doing practice for someone is one thing, but if the person has an empty stomach, we need to feed them. If they are sick, we need to give them medicine. Meditating on food won't feed them. Go and take action.

Our practice really needs to be in action. In the early days, in the seventh or eighth century, all the practice was in meditation and prayer. But today, that is not enough. Practice needs to be applied in action in society. If we don't put the practice into action, the practice does not have much value. We don't have to wait for enlightenment to do something good for another person. We have the capability to do this now. This way, our practice is more meaningful and gives a result.

22. How to Subdue Inner Wildness

དགུ་པ་སྟོང་བ་ལམ་ཁྱེར་ནི།
Ninth, uniting with the path:

རང་གི་དུག་ལྔའི་དགྲ་བོ་མ་ཐུལ་ན།
If I cannot subdue my own [inner] enemies of the five poisons,

ཕ་རོལ་དགྲ་ནི་འདལ་ཞིང་འཐེལ་བར་འགྱུར།
Then outer enemies will increase and may be pervasive.

དེ་ཕྱིར་གནས་ལུགས་ཆེན་པོ་སྙིང་རྗེའི་དམག
Therefore, the army of compassion of the great abiding nature

རང་སེམས་འཁྲུལ་པའི་དགྲ་རྣམས་ཐུལ་བར་གྱུར།
Will subdue the illusory enemies of the mind.

Within each of us are our own enemies: ignorance, anger, pride, jealousy, and attachment. If we are unable to conquer these internal enemies, then it will be futile to attempt to subdue other enemies in the world.

This, too, is a very practical instruction. If there is a problem, we normally look at the external conditions. If someone makes us angry or upset, we might look at that situation and try to control that condition or person.

But the bothered and upset feeling we have in these circumstances arises from our internal selves—not from anything external. The external phenomena are just a temporal condition that allows us to manifest our inner five poisons.

The external condition is just a condition; it is not the emotion itself. The grain of barley can only grow if it has the external conditions of water, heat, and soil. External conditions are like that. They help the seed of anger grow, but the initial seed of that anger is within us.

The text says the inner five poisons are the most powerful enemy. Each of these five poisons is our main enemy. Our anger is the greatest danger to ourselves. It can destroy us. The same is true with jealousy, attachment, and ignorance. We don't experience these from the outside. We experience them within our body and mind. We may have a physical reaction; our face may become red, or our body may shake. We may not be in control of our speech, and we may use harsh words. We may lose control of our emotions and actions. We may not even realize how fast our inner consciousness violently reacts to the conditions. We only realize after it is over, and we wonder how that outburst could happen. This shows how powerful this inner energy and anger can be. Once it is outside us, it can't be taken back, so it can cause great pain for oneself and others.

In the 7th century, one of the great Zhang Zhung masters, Nangzher Lodpo, was asked by one of his close disciples what was most important for controlling our inner enemy. He said to control your own inner enemy, control your own mind, because it's only one. If you try to control the outer enemies, you won't be able to, because there are too many. If you can control yourself, then you can control all the outside enemies as well.

Basically, what this means is that we should control our own energies and emotions. The main enemy is the five poisons. Even if we overcome our outer enemy, if we overcome the challenges of the external person, it does not mean we have overcome the five poisons, because there will always be more external conditions to deal with.

We must pay close attention to our practice so that we will realize when the emotion begins to manifest. Then it is easier to control. If we can control the smoke before it breaks out into flames, it is easier to control. If we remain mindful, then we can see the emotion beginning to arise and apply the practice to control it. Doing this, it will never manifest outward in a large way. But if we follow after the emotion, we make it worse.

To subdue the fire of anger, we need to apply the water of kindness, calmness, and simplicity. The antidote of anger is kindness (Tib. *jampa*). This is what we need to practice. By doing this, we learn patience and have the capacity to hold things with patience. This is how we can grow productively when we experience challenges.

23. How to Overcome Attachment

བཅུ་པ་ཆགས་པ་ལམ་བྱེར་ནི།
Tenth, ways to put attachment onto the path:

འདོད་ཆགས་ཡོན་ཏན་ལན་ཚྭའི་ཆུ་དང་མཚུངས།
The qualities of attachment are like salty water.

ཇི་ཙམ་སྤྱད་ཅིང་འདོད་པ་ཕྱིར་ཕྱིར་འཕེལ།
The more we drink, the more we crave.

གང་ལ་ཆགས་ཞེན་སྐྱེས་པའི་དངོས་པོ་ཀུན།
All things toward which attachment and clinging arise—

འཕལ་དུ་སྤང་ནས་ཆོག་ཤེས་གཏེར་ལ་སྦྱོད།
Abandon them immediately and experience the treasure of contentment.

In Tibetan, the term *död chag* means desire and attachment. *Död* means desire, and *chag* means attachment. It is not healthy to be too attached to things. It causes us to only want more and more. If we learn to let go by sharing with others, it will be much more meaningful, and we will experience the joy of inner satisfaction.

The example in this stanza is very clear. Drinking salty water is not the way to overcome thirst. If we are very thirsty, it may momentarily soothe the thirst, but it will actually increase our thirst.

The more we are attached, the more we want. This means we are not looking back and saying, "I have enough, I'm okay, I'm happy with what I have."

Desire leads to attachment. At first, we may have a desire for something. Unchecked, this creates more and more energy until we really want that thing. That wanting continues to increase until we are completely attached to what we desire.

We may not even realize how we become attached. With all the new technology and material luxuries, there is always something new to desire.

The monks in training are also human beings. They have desires too. They are no different from other people, except they train themselves and may have better understanding. His Holiness, the 33rd sMenri Trizin, was very wise in helping us detach from these new things. He would always tell us not to worry about them because, "A better model will come out later, this one isn't very good."

Our attachment has no end. We keep running after new technology, and it will never end. We need to learn to break that habit, knowing that we can survive just fine without these things. We should take advantage of the technology but not become dependent on it. If we become dependent on it, we push ourselves further and further into the material world, and we will not be able to benefit from our natural abilities.

Detachment pulls us back from the material world and allows us stand on our own two feet. Our life can function perfectly if we rely on ourselves. But we must be happy with where we are first, meaning we don't have any complaints, and we are satisfied. Because we are lacking this satisfaction, our attachment never ends.

Additionally, just because we are attached, does not mean we will always get what we want. Instead, we might just exhaust ourselves running after things. So, we need to know how to slow down and rest in the experience of contentment and satisfaction.

24. Non-Dual Contemplation

གཉིས་པ་དོན་དམ་བྱང་ཆུབ་སེམས་ལ་གཉིས་ལས། ༈

Second [meditation on enlightened mind], the ultimate mind of enlightenment has two parts:

དང་པོ་མཉམ་བཞག་སྤྲོས་བྲལ་འཛིན་མེད་སྒོམ་པ་ནི།

First, meditative equipoise without conceptual fabrication or grasping:

ཉིན་མཚན་སྣང་བ་མ་ལུས་རང་གི་སེམས།

All appearances of day and night are one's own mind.

སེམས་ཉིད་མ་བཅོས་གནས་ལུགས་མཐའ་དང་བྲལ།

The uncontrived abiding Nature of Mind is free from extremes.

དེ་ཉིད་ཤེས་ན་གཟུང་འཛིན་མདུད་པ་གྲོལ།

If one understands this principle, the knots of subject and object are released.

དེ་བཞིན་སྤྲོས་བྲལ་འཛིན་མེད་སེམས་ལ་ལྟོས།

In this way, look on the [nondual] mind, unconditioned and without grasping.

Ultimately, through the practice, we can come to see the visions of day and night, of everything we experience, as generated from our own mind, which is boundless. Once we realize that the human mind has such capabilities, we can contemplate and look at things with a clear view, seeing things as they truly are.

This stanza is about non-dual contemplation. While we try to meditate in this way, it does not mean we always can. We are a mixture of all the things we are experiencing within ourselves—the things we're chasing after or the new things we are planning. Even if we sit for one hour every day in meditation, this does not necessarily mean we are truly meditating.

In Tibetan, this contemplation is called *Nyam Shag*. It means being able to leave everything as it is and remain undistracted in that state. In this state, we are contemplating with no effect from our illusionary thought.

Even just a moment of experiencing this state is a moment of non-dual meditation. We need to practice this. This is true Nature of Mind we talk about in Bön. The unmodified Nature of Mind is measureless. According to Dho (Skt. Sutra), we say "emptiness." In Ngag (Skt. Tantra) and Dzogchen, we say *Tigle Nangchik*, the single-pointed Nature of Mind.

The Nature of Mind has no limit; there is no way to measure it. Therefore, it is measureless. This also means it is very open and spacious. Everything can manifest within the space of that nature. If we realize this, we will be free. When we realize the true Nature of Mind, we are totally free. There is ultimate freedom found in that experience of contemplating in the non-dual state or our natural state of mind. For as long as we are there, we are totally free—free from ego, free from ignorance, free from any and all defilements that arise through our emotions.

Within that freedom, spontaneous manifestations arise. All sorts of things spontaneously arise—good and bad thoughts, big and small thoughts, colorful and black-and-white thoughts.

Everything spontaneously arises, but we are not being affected by what is arising. We are still contemplating in the natural state of mind. When we are clearly in that state, we are free from the concepts of subject and object.

Right now, our way of perceiving things is as "self" and "other." We feel these are two separate things. This is an illusion. When we can contemplate on the Nature of Mind, we cross beyond the boundary of subject and object. *Rigpa* and the Nature of Mind are unified in ultimate essence. We can no longer say that something is divided into subject and object. The state is beyond that.

Then, automatically, there arises both cyclic existence and the enlightened state—*khorwa* and *nyang dhe* (Skt. *samsara* and *nirvana*). In Dzogchen, khorwa is not a negative and nyang dhe is not something up in heaven. They're both in one nature. It is only our ordinary mind that looks at them as two dimensions. We think that nirvana is so pure. We think that khorwa is so polluted. But that is just how we perceive things. It doesn't mean that is how it truly is.

Therefore, in the Dzogchen teaching, it says that the moment we realize our Nature of Mind is the moment we are enlightened. If we don't realize it, we are deluded and in khorwa. So, the only difference between khorwa and nyang dhe is discovering and non-discovering—or realizing and non-realizing. There is no real gap between them.

Remaining in non-dual contemplation frees us from emotional grasping at subject and object—as well as concepts of self and other. Grasping is automatically released, because we are no longer holding things as a subject or an object. Ultimately, the nature of all things is the same in essence—the nature of emptiness.

So, contemplate and look non-dually into your mind. Looking into your Rigpa, contemplate your Nature of Mind. That is your enlightened world. Realize it, experience it, and have the results of that realization. Discover and keep contemplating. This is the process of training and stabilizing your contemplation. Eventually, you will gain experience, and you will receive the result of that experience.

In Tibetan, we say *Nyam Tog*. *Nyam* means experience; *Tog* means discovery or realizing. When we realize things, it is wonderful. But if we don't practice continually, we will not reach into the experience and will not be able to have the results. Simply realizing doesn't help very much. It's only good at that very moment. It's like knowing one person, very briefly, but then no longer having a connection to them. The feeling we have about that person does not last very long. Soon, we forget them. If we see that person again, we may not even realize that we are familiar with them.

When we realize the true Nature of Mind once, it needs to be practiced again and again. We must continually meditate on it. The Tibetan word for this is *gom*. The English translation is "meditation" although it more closely translates to "familiarity" or "to familiarize." We are making ourselves familiar with that realization.

If we get to know someone well, we become familiar with their style of acting and speaking, and the way they look. The

ACTUAL PRACTICE

moment we think of them, we have a picture of them in our mind. They may invoke a certain feeling in us. We don't even need to put much more energy into it. We just think of them, and we know them.

This is the same way with the realization of the Nature of Mind. Realizing it once doesn't help—don't be satisfied with that. Your teacher can introduce you to your Nature of Mind, giving you a realization once, but if you don't continue practicing, you will not have stability of that realization. It is easily diminished, because our ego and ignorance is so active and powerful, it can take us away from true realization.

25. Understanding the Truthlessness of Pleasantness

གཉིས་པ་ཡིད་འོང་མི་འོང་སྡུག་བསྔལ་དང་གསུམ་སྟེ། ༈

Second [part of the ultimate mind of enlightenment], the three categories of pleasantness, unpleasantness, and suffering:

དང་པོ་ཡིད་འོང་བདེན་ཞེན་སྤོངས་པ་ནི།

First, abandoning attachment to pleasantness as truly existing:

ཡིད་འོང་མཛེས་ལྗགས་ཡུལ་དང་འཕྲད་པ་ན།

When one encounters a beautiful and attractive object,

དབྱར་གྱི་འཇའ་བཞིན་ཁ་དོག་ལེགས་ན་ཡང་།

With beautiful colors like a rainbow in the summer,

གནས་ལུགས་རྟོགས་རྟོགས་བདེན་པ་མེད་རེས་མཐོང་།

By realizing the natural state, one sees with certainty its truthlessness.

དེས་ན་ཆགས་ཞེན་སྤངས་པའི་དོན་ཀུན་ཤེས།

Therefore, one knows the meaning of abandoning all attachment.

The things that our dualistic minds love most, the things we hold most dear, are only ours for a moment—like a rainbow in the summer—and then they are gone. We naturally grasp at things we find pleasant, but we should not. Instead, we should work to understand the true nature of their existence.

We attach to what we like most. We hold it like we are glued to it. To relieve that grasping, how do we apply the teaching in a practical way?

We often see beautiful rainbows. People like to take photos of them. When we see a rainbow, we may feel calmer or happier; something may change inside of us. But we never think that we can take the rainbow home with us. We never think that we could hold onto it. We know it is not possible. The rainbow is beautiful, but when we try to get close, it moves away. We know that what we see does not truly materially exist. That is the clear example given here.

Now apply this concept to the rest of the material world. It is all just like a rainbow—everything looks beautiful and perfect and solid, but it is not solid, it is just as temporary as a rainbow. So, there is no reason to try to hold or grasp onto things, because they will never be truly solid.

This stanza emphasizes the need to realize the natural state. We need to learn the truthlessness of the material world—to learn that the material world does not exist in the way we perceive it. It is all just temporary, so we need to subdue this kind of "everlasting grasping." The Tibetan term *dzinpa* means self-holding the "I" or "me." When we are able to release it, then we are free. For example, when we hold our hand in a fist, the hand is tight. When we open our hand, there is more freedom. Similarly, we become free of the holding and grasping caused by our own ignorance when we practice and realize the natural state of our mind.

Normally, we see everything as solid, and we instinctually tie it to us as a solid thing. We must learn how to detach from this. We understand the truthlessness of things by realizing the true nature.

We do not hold an attachment to the rainbow, because we know it is not practical to do so. If we can release our attachment to a rainbow, why can't we release our attachment to certain objects? It is very simple. We just have to see it the same as a rainbow, a dream, or a mirage.

Everything is all just a name; everything exists by its name or symbol. Nothing is solid, nothing is independent, and nothing is inherent. But we grab everything we are attached to in the opposite way—as if it were solid, independent, and concrete. That is the fault and weakness of our wisdom, and the strong energy of ignorance. Through practice, we can correctly understand the truthlessness of these things.

26. Understanding the Truthlessness of Unpleasantness

གཉིས་པ་ཡིད་དུ་མི་འོང་བ་ལ་བདེན་ཞེན་སྤོང་བ་ནི།

Second, abandoning emotional grasping to unpleasantness as truly existing:

ཡིད་དུ་མི་འོང་མི་གཙང་ཡུལ་འཕྲད་པར།

When encountering unpleasant and impure things,

རང་སེམས་འཁྲུལ་ལ་བདེན་པ་མེད་ཤེས་ཤིང་།

Knowing that this is truthless and a delusion of one's own mind.

ཁྱི་ཕག་འདྲ་བའི་གད་ལའང་གཙང་རྟོག་མེད།

Like for a dog or a pig, for whom nothing is ugly or pure,

གསེར་དངུལ་ས་རྡོ་ཕྱད་མེད་སེམས་ཀྱིས་མཐོང་།

Mentally perceive gold and silver, and earth and stone, without any selective differentiation.

The previous stanza talked about the truthlessness of things you like. This stanza talks about the truthlessness of things you do not like. Equally, both are inherently non-existent. They are both truthless.

It is because of our own inner projections that we choose to dislike someone or something. We need to realize that our feelings about people, places, and things are an unconscious act of the mind. Most of the time, our minds are unable to see that all things are equal in essence. This stanza is saying that, just as the dog and pig do not distinguish between clean and dirty, likewise our mind should realize that, in essence, there is no real difference between things like a piece of beautiful gold and a simple dirty stone.

Any so-called suffering or feeling of dislike will not last forever. It is only momentary. It may only last a day. Even something that we dislike today may be something we like next week. Similarly, suffering is only momentary. Suffering can be healed and transformed; it can be removed. We must accept that suffering and unpleasantness is a part of life, with every possibility of change and transformation. Today there is suffering, tomorrow there is happiness; or today there is happiness and tomorrow there is sadness. Everything is impermanent; everything is like a dream; everything is like a rainbow.

We should try to be like a child who does things spontaneously. With no sense of good or bad, children just play happily. They have no sense that the playground they are on may be dirty; they just have spontaneous character. Our normal pretending character is actually more of our ignorance, while our spontaneous character is truer.

In the higher teachings of Dzogchen, we give an example: The more you become a Dzogchen yogi or *Naljorpa*, the more you become like a child—in the sense of personality, flexibility, emotional freedom, and lack of grasping. Many masters are like that. They are free from the concept of what people think or don't think of them. They act spontaneously. They are free from any worry or concept of thinking what's good or bad.

They can sometimes seem to be careless people, as they don't seem to care about food or how they dress. They only care about practice. Their greatest joy is simply being in the natural state of mind. Because they have been totally freed from the concept of good and bad, they are free from being bothered. This is what it truly means to cut through delusions.

The last two lines of this stanza give the example of dogs and pigs, and gold and stone. When we realize the truthlessness of liking and disliking, then we have no concept of selective attitude. Like dogs and pigs have no concept of what is either gold and silver, or stone and dirt, we must have this realization of their truthlessness to be free from the concepts of positive and negative, good and bad.

27. Understanding the Truthlessness of Suffering

གསུམ་པ་སྡུག་བསྔལ་ལ་བདེན་ཞེན་སྤང་བ་ནི།
Third, abandoning emotional grasping to suffering as truly existing:

སྡུག་བསྔལ་སྣ་ཚོགས་རྨི་ལམ་ལྟ་བུ་ལ།
The varieties of suffering are like a dream.

བདེན་པར་བཟུང་བ་ཤིན་ཏུ་འཁྲུལ་པ་སྟེ།
Grasping them as true is an extreme delusion.

མི་མཐུན་རྐྱེན་ངན་ཡུལ་དང་འཕྲད་པའི་ཚེ།
When encountering adverse conditions or objects in this life,

རང་སྣང་འཁྲུལ་པ་བདེན་པར་མ་གྲུབ་བོ།
See them as illusionary appearances and not truly existent.

Suffering, like a dream, lives only as an illusion in our mind. If, and when, we face calamity or disaster of any kind, we should realize it as a projection of our own illusionary thoughts and as free from inherent existence.

As a practitioner, if we are going through a long illness, we should not feel disappointed by it. Instead, apply the illness as a tool to enter the path of enlightenment. Our suffering from illness can be transformed into practice. We say, "transforming it into the path."

We can also think that we are taking on the suffering of all other sentient beings to free them of their suffering. By these methods, we can reduce our own outer feeling of suffering. We can diminish the suffering experience by the power of our contemplation and ability to transform our suffering into the path. This is part of the practice of the mind of enlightenment. By doing this, our suffering is not the suffering of our own self. We transform the suffering into a practice tool that can be for healing all beings.

People are usually angry, afraid, or upset by suffering. But just like pleasantness and unpleasantness, suffering is all part of illusion. Not realizing that suffering is truthless causes us to have more suffering, because we hold onto it. Instead, we should take on the suffering of others, dedicate our practice for them, think of them positively, and wish for their healing, so that our suffering may be of benefit.

When we are going through bad pain, we can look at the suffering itself. Meditate on the specific pain. Meditate on who is experiencing that pain. Just look into it. By looking at who is suffering—who is experiencing that so-called suffering—and by contemplating on the suffering itself, we begin to go into the real nature of that suffering.

Suffering and the nature of suffering are two different things. Suffering itself is physical, and we sense it on a gross level. We can feel it. The outer pain is a manifestation of our ignorance or of karma. But inner suffering or pain is because of our thought, which we hold or grasp onto, causing us to feel it more.

The nature of suffering is not visible but can be experienced and noticed inwardly. So, don't look only at the suffering itself but look deeply into it—at the nature of the suffering. Enter into that very nature of suffering, and you will move beyond the outer suffering. You will be able to overcome the pain and enter into a new experience. That new experience is the nature of the pain or suffering you're going through.

You can experiment with this on yourself. It is something that many masters have gone through. The power of true meditation can transform the pain. Everyone has the potential to do it, but you must believe in it. This is how we transform suffering. We should not look at suffering as simply suffering, because then it seems like it is solid and concrete. Instead, understand it as the text says—as just an ignorant projection of your own mind.

Nothing is everlasting. Pain can be changed, it can be healed, and comfort will come naturally. Release your grasp of pain and suffering and use this as a path of practice.

28. Practice of Generosity

གསུམ་པ་དེ་དག་གི་བསླབ་བྱ་ལ་ལྔ། ༈

Third [way to liberate from the extremes of the cyclic world and enlightenment], there are the five points of advice:

དང་པོ་ཕ་རོལ་ཕྱིན་པ་དྲུག་ལ་བསླབ་པའི་དང་པོ་སྦྱིན་པའི་ཕ་རོལ་ཕྱིན་པ་ནི།

The first [point of advice] is the Six Transcendental Practices, [beginning with] the practice of generosity:

བྱང་ཆུབ་རྟེན་ལ་ལུས་སྲོག་གཏོང་ཞེས་པས།

Give up one's life and body for the sake of enlightenment,

རྒྱན་གོས་ཟས་ནོར་ལོངས་སྤྱོད་དབང་ཐང་ལ།

[Including] ornaments, clothing, food, wealth, possessions, power, and so forth,

སེར་སྣ་ཆགས་ཞེན་མེད་པའི་སྦྱིན་པ་ནི།

Giving without any attachment or miserliness.

ཕ་རོལ་འགྲོ་ལ་གང་འདོད་རྒྱུན་དུ་གཏོང་།

Continuously give to other beings whatever they desire.

This stanza advises that we follow the Six Transcendental Practices to obtain an enlightened mind. The first of these practices is Generosity.

To be truly generous, we must give what we have to anyone—friend and foe alike—with no thought of reward for the act. Giving generously means giving unconditionally without any ulterior motive.

We often think that generosity means giving wealth, and that if someone has wealth, they can be generous. People think that if they do not have wealth, they cannot practice generosity. It is not always like that.

We can categorize generosity in three ways according to a text on the subject: the Generosity of Teaching (*Bön gyi Jinpa*); the Generosity of Protection (*Kyab kyi Jinpa*); and the Generosity of Material Goods (*Sang Sing gyi Jinpa*). These are the three major generosities.

Generosity can be practiced as in the Dho teachings of Tönpa Shenrab. Whenever Tönpa Shenrab traveled for a teaching, he instructed his disciples to practice generosity, morality, concentration, enthusiasm, contemplation, and wisdom realization, because these are all very important.

These transcendental practices are important for Ngag and Dzogchen practitioners as well. Some people think that if they are a Dzogchen practitioner, they do not need all these recitation prayers and basic practices—they don't need all these six (sometimes listed as ten) transcendental practices, because they just need to contemplate in the natural state. While it is true that if we can contemplate directly in the state of realization, we don't depend on these practices from the point of view of the Nature. This is true from the perspective of contemplating on Dzogchen view. But this does not mean that Dzogchenpa (practitioners) do not need these practices. It's important to understand the difference. To reach that level, these transcendental practices are essential. Otherwise, Sangye Tönpa Shenrab would never have taught them. They are the ultimate support or condition for successful practice and are needed to generate a true mind of enlightenment.

We say that for a bird to fly to its destination, it needs both wings to be healthy. It will not work only having one healthy wing. In the same way, we are working to achieve the mind of enlightenment. To do so, these relative supports or conditions of the transcendental practices are needed.

The first of these practices is generosity. One of the main weaknesses of human beings is a lack of generosity—not just the intention of generosity, but the action of generosity. We easily say, "I would like to be generous and give," but when it comes to action, we may question whether we should give things or not, or if we should wait. If we think in this way, we still have attachment and will not achieve the wisdom of the generosity. This is ignorance. Attachment destroys the achievement of realization, so generosity is important.

The first major generosity is giving time and energy through teaching—giving knowledge without attachment, holding back, or grasping on it. Through this, we can lead someone to the path of enlightenment. We can lead someone to understand the true nature of their own mind or at least help someone understand the differences between virtuous and non-virtuous deeds.

His Holiness, the 33rd late sMenri Trizin and His Eminence, Yongdzin Rinpoche were living examples of this, always ready to teach—they were even hesitant to give us a day off! Giving the

Generosity of Teaching is the greatest generosity. It must be given through pure motivation.

In my book, *Opening the Door to Bön*, I mentioned the proper qualities of the teacher. Many texts talk about what students must do, but few talk about the qualities needed for a proper teacher. According to Tönpa Shenrab's teaching, the teacher has a huge responsibility. A qualified teacher must keep a certain sense of morality, otherwise he or she will not be qualified according to Bön. The teacher must give of the teaching, any time and anywhere it is needed.

The second type of generosity is of rescue and protection. If someone is sick, we can help them get to a doctor or hospital and buy medicine. If someone's life is in danger, we can protect them. In Tibetan culture, we also have the tradition of saving animals' lives—fish, birds, sheep, or yak. We release them in the name of someone who is sick or in the name of our teacher. Or in general, for the sake of saving someone's life, they are freed with a ceremony, and we dedicate the release. This is called a *Tse Thar*.

The third major generosity is material generosity, which we all know—giving to people anything they need without hesitation or attachment.

29. Practice of Morality

གཉིས་པ་ཚུལ་ཁྲིམས་བར་ཕྱིན་ནི།

Second [transcendental practice], the practice of morality:

ལྟ་བ་ནམ་མཁའ་དག་དང་མཉམ་ན་ཡང་།

Even if one's [meditational] view is [vast] like the sky,

སྤྱོད་པ་མི་ལ་བསྟུན་ཏེ་ཚུལ་ཁྲིམས་སྲུང་།

One's conduct should be in accord with moral character suitable to mankind.

ཚུལ་ཁྲིམས་མེད་པས་རང་གཞན་དོན་མི་འགྲུབ།

Without ethical behavior, one will not accomplish their own or others' aims.

འཆལ་མེད་ཚུལ་ཁྲིམས་རྒྱུན་དུ་བསྲུང་བར་བྱ།

One should continuously maintain uncorrupted moral discipline.

In our day-to-day life, it is important to act morally and treat all of mankind with dignity and respect. If we do not act morally, our life will not be as fulfilled, and we will lose self-worth and respect. It is important to achieve this goal for ourselves and others.

Even if our meditational view is as vast as the sky, no matter how high our level of realization, we are still a human being. Our characteristic behavior must be suitable to the society we live in. We must not be destructive or disturb others in that society. We should not act like we have achieved some high realization, pretending to be something we're not. People would be bothered by this. This develops a negative concept for people to the tradition, and it becomes negative karma that we would cultivate because of our character. This is why the stanza says that even if our meditational view is very high, we are bound by morality and ethics. All our conduct should be suitable to society—just like any ordinary person.

Don't go beyond the morality of society. Don't think we practitioners are above anyone else. Otherwise, we may develop negative karma. Live in harmony with those around us. That is what this text means.

30. Practice of Patience

གསུམ་པ་བཟོད་པའི་ཕར་ཕྱིན་ནི།

Third [transcendental practice], the practice of patience:

བླ་མེད་བྱང་ཆུབ་སྒྲུབ་པའི་སྐྱེས་བུ་ལ།

To those who are on path to achieve highest enlightenment,

གནོད་བྱེད་ཐམས་ཅད་རིན་ཆེན་གཏེར་དང་མཚུངས།

All harm and destruction are like a treasure of jewels.

གང་ལ་ཡང་སེམས་སྙིང་རྗེའི་དཔུང་བསྐྱེད་ནས།

Generate the force of compassion, having an attitude of benefiting others.

དགྲ་གཉེན་ཀུན་ལ་བཟོད་པའི་གོ་ཆ་གྱོན།

Wear the armor of patience for both friends and foes in all places.

If we are trying to reach ultimate perfection and happiness, we should consider each obstacle that confronts us as a positive, not a negative. To do this, observe patiently, without negative reaction, and it will be like finding a treasure of jewels in the path, because it provides us with a wonderful opportunity to apply our practice.

Any struggle in the path of practice, and any challenges or difficulties, should be seen as precious jewels. Precious jewels have the quality to grant energy and benefit through healing or the fulfilling of wishes. Challenges on the path of practice should be seen as jewels because these challenges strengthen and teach us to apply the practice and give us an opportunity for practice. Therefore, these are not obstacles; they should be seen with respect—as precious.

As I mentioned before, disasters should not be always seen as negative. Look at them in a positive way because of the wisdom you can gain from them too. They allow you to manifest your inner quality of wisdom, love, and compassion. Going through such struggles will give you the patience to practice. This becomes wisdom and the positive energy that develops your inner state of realization. So, by practicing genuinely and patiently, it energizes you and gives you the strength of wisdom and compassion, unconditionally.

Everyone has conditional compassion. But unconditional compassion is very rare. We need to always practice patience if we are to understand unconditional compassion.

31. Practice of Diligence

བཞི་པ་བརྩོན་འགྲུས་པར་ཕྱིན་ནི།

Fourth [transcendental practice], the practice of diligence:

ཉིན་མཚན་ཀུན་ཏུ་ཐར་ལམ་སྒྲུབ་པ་ལ།

To always practice the path of liberation—day and night,

སྐྲ་ལ་མེ་ཤོར་ལྟ་བུར་བརྩོན་མཆོད་ནས།

Have diligence, like someone putting out a fire in their hair.

འགྲོ་དོན་སྒྲུབ་འདོད་ཡོན་ཏན་འབྱུང་གནས་ཀྱི།

The intention to achieve benefit for beings is the source of all good qualities.

རྣམ་དཀར་དགེ་བའི་ལས་ལ་བརྩོན་འགྲུས་སྐྱེད།

Develop enthusiastic effort in all virtuous actions.

At all times, day and night, a person must engage in virtuous deeds and practice the art of effort and continuous diligence to benefit all sentient beings.

Regularity of practice, or diligence in your practice, means practicing without postponing and practicing regularly. Regularity in practice is very important. Once in a while, we might have a special inspiration because of the place where we are practicing. Or we may have inspiration from the teacher we meet. If we don't follow that inspiration regularly, then that interest will gradually decrease, and we will soon find an excuse to postpone our practice. We may even totally give up.

So, the text says we need to enthusiastically put our energy into regular practice like someone with fire in their hair. Will they wait even a moment before trying to put it out? No, they will put all their energy and effort toward putting it out until they are sure the fire is gone. This is the level of effort the text is calling for us to put toward our meditation and toward performing virtuous actions for other beings.

So, even if it is only a short practice, we need to practice regularly. Make it a habitual pattern; make it a part of your regular day. You can think of it like needing your coffee in the morning so that you can wake up. Or needing a shower before you go to bed so that you can sleep. Adopt it as part of your regular day in your mind, body, and energy. By making it a regular part of your day, your progress increases.

32. Practice of Concentration

བསམ་གཏན་ཕར་ཕྱིན་ནི།

Fifth [transcendental practice], the practice of concentration:

ཞི་བའི་གནས་ལ་ཡེ་ཤེས་ལྷག་གི་མཐོང་།

By abiding in a state of inner peace, one can clearly see wisdom.

འཁོར་བའི་མུན་སེལ་ཤེས་བྱའི་དཀྱིལ་འཁོར་རྒྱས།

The Kyil Khor (Skt. Mandala) of knowledge expands, dispelling the darkness of cyclic existence.

གཟུགས་མེད་བཞི་ལས་ཡང་དག་འདས་པ་ཡི།

The four formless states are completely transcended.

གཡོ་རྟོག་དེ་དགས་མེད་པའི་བསམ་གཏན་བསྒོམ།

Meditate with concentration, without wavering, free from doubt.

Once we have reached the state of inner peace, we must continue to practice with concentration. To meditate effectively, we must approach the practice with a clear mind that is devoid of any expectations or doubts. When we achieve this, we will have gone above the four formless states, eliminated ignorance, and expanded wisdom.

Concentration is important. When we lack concentration and focus during our meditation or in our day-to-day lives, it affects other areas of our life. We need good focus in our relationships. We need good focus in our profession. We need good focus while raising children.

In the practice, the more we have focus, the more we have stability and clarity in our meditative experience. When we have proper practice without distraction, we have stability and clarity in our meditative experience. When we have a good experience with good stability, we can remain longer with any practice without distraction.

If we lack concentration, staying in meditation for two hours does not mean we have actually practiced for two hours. We may have only truly practiced for five or ten minutes. The rest of the time, we are in and out, in and out.

Additionally, we must ensure our meditation is not influenced by wildness or agitation, nor let it be dull or sleepy. We need to watch ourselves even if we are practicing regularly. Agitation is easy to notice. When experiencing it, we know right away that we are not concentrating or focusing well. But *mugpa* and *thipa*, dullness and sleepiness, are harder to distinguish. We may be meditating but without the full energy of concentration. When there is no energy of meditation, there is no growth of wisdom, no growth of realization, no growth of clarity. There is no joy of achieving the stability of the Zhine experience. We may be comfortable physically but mentally disturbed in the practice.

We need to build up the stability of concentration. By building up our concentration in practice, it helps generate the clarity of wisdom. This automatically eliminates the darkness of ignorance and lets the light of wisdom arise. The light of wisdom is clarity. Clear and true concentration with wisdom is free from doubt and confusion. Without having any doubts or confusion, our meditation is clear and precise. We will know exactly what we are practicing and will remain stable and focused. And then our practice time is never wasted.

33. Practice of Wisdom

ཤེས་རབ་ཕར་ཕྱིན་ནི།

Sixth [transcendental practice], the practice of wisdom:

ཕ་རོལ་ཕྱིན་ལྔ་སྨོས་ཏུ་མོད་ན་ཡང་།

Although the five transcendental practices have been mentioned,

རྟོགས་སངས་རྒྱས་འདོད་སྨྱིས་མཆོག་ཐབས་མཁས་པས།

The skillful means of great masters and [those who] aspire for perfect enlightenment,

འཁོར་གསུམ་མི་རྟོག་ཤེས་རབ་ཕ་རོལ་ཕྱིན།

Is Ultimate Wisdom, the non-conceptualization (or true realization) of the three spheres (subject, action, and object),

བླ་མེད་ཡང་དག་བདག་མེད་མཐའ་བྲལ་རྟོགས།

The unsurpassable realization of perfect selflessness, free from extremes.

This stanza tells us that the previous five transcendental practices are important, but wisdom is what leads to realization. With ultimate wisdom, one realizes the true nature of all existence and understands that self does not inherently exist as we perceive it.

The previous stanzas referred to the first five of the ten transcendental practices. This is the sixth *Parchin Chu*—wisdom. Wisdom cuts the root of ignorance. Wisdom totally frees us from ignorance. If we have the wisdom of realization, then we have the wisdom of being free from ignorance.

Cutting the root of ignorance is cutting the root of suffering. True realization of wisdom of your own self cuts the boundary of dependency; it cuts the boundary of materialism. The true wisdom of realization is just clear, energetic presence within the integration of the natural state of mind and awareness, Rigpa itself. That is true wisdom, like a bright, shining sun with no clouds. When the bright sun is shining in the sky, there is no moment of darkness or non-clarity. Wisdom is like that. When there is no doubt or darkness, then there is no suffering. You are free from it. That is why we say that wisdom "cuts the root of suffering."

34. Searching Your Own Delusions

གཉིས་པ་མདོ་ནས་གསུངས་པའི་བོན་བཞི་ལ་བསླབ་པས། ༈

Second [of the five points of advice], training according to the Four Bön, according to the text:

དང་པོ་རང་གི་འཁྲུལ་བར་བརྟགས་ནས་སྤོང་པ་ནི།

First, renunciation by examining one's own delusion:

རང་སྣང་འཁྲུལ་རྒྱུན་རང་གིས་མ་བལྟས་ན།

If one doesn't look to the source of their own deluded perceptions,

ཆོས་པའི་གཟུགས་ཀྱིས་ཆོས་མིན་བྱེད་སྲིད་པས།

It is possible to perform non-spiritual actions in the guise of a practitioner.

རྣམ་པ་ཀུན་ཏུ་རང་གི་འཁྲུལ་པ་ལ།

Look at one's own delusions in every moment.

བློས་ནས་འཁྲུལ་པའི་སྐྱོན་རྣམས་མ་ལུས་དོར།

In this way, all the faults of delusion are abandoned.

We need to search our own illusionary thoughts carefully and diligently. Ascertain whether these thoughts and perceptions are deluded or spiritual. We must renounce the delusions we do not find to be spiritual and investigate the source of our misperception.

Even if we are a good and regular practitioner, and a very spiritual person, it is important to occasionally reflect on ourselves. We need to look at ourselves and our understanding in regular life. Are our thoughts deluded? Did we not understand what was told to us? Was our understanding based on our emotions? If we realize we are deluded, we must put effort toward denouncing that delusion.

As a yogi, it is still possible to perform actions that are against the teaching. It is even possible to perform negative, non-spiritual actions in the name of being a practitioner. This is contradictory. Deluded action can harm others. This is why we must always look at our own delusions. When we see that our view or action is incorrect, we must correct it.

35. Avoiding Meaningless Talk

གཉིས་པ་སྨྲ་བ་སྤང་པ་ནི།
Second, renunciation of meaningless talk:

ཐེག་པ་ཆེན་པོར་ཞུགས་པའི་གང་ཟག་གིས།
Even for a practitioner of the greater vehicle,

སྨྲ་བ་མང་ན་བསམ་པ་འཁྲུལ་བར་འགྱུར།
If one talks a lot, their thoughts will be deluded.

བདག་གཞན་བཟང་ངན་ཅིར་ཡང་མི་བརྗོད་པར།
Without commenting on the good or bad of self or others,

སྒྲ་བསམ་བརྗོད་མེད་མ་བཅོས་མཉམ་པར་བཞག
Contemplate the unmodified state, without speech, thought, or expression.

Earlier we talked about gossiping. Here the text is saying that we, as a practitioner, should not waste our time talking excessively and meaninglessly. Instead of wasting our time in idle talk, we should put our time into active meditation, so we will be able to gain something from our time.

Some people say they don't have time to practice meditation, even for a few minutes, but then spend many hours of the day gossiping or speaking without purpose. This doesn't make much sense, especially for someone who is considered a practitioner. We should not speak without any goal or benefit to come from it. Even if we don't want to meditate, we can instead at least recite some prayers or Nyenpa.

See gossiping and idle speech as a weakness to overcome. If you can instead focus your energy of speech on reciting Nyenpa, you will have a greater ability to focus your mind.

36. Detaching from Materialism

གསུམ་པ་སྦྱིན་བདག་སོགས་ཀྱི་ཁྱིམ་ལ་ཆགས་ཞེན་སྤང་བ་ནི།

Third, renunciation of attachment to the home and benefactors:

འཁོར་བའི་ཁྱིམ་ལ་འཁོར་བའི་ལས་སྒྲིབ་དེས།

Because of the karmic obscurations of [living in] a worldly home,

ཐོས་བསམ་བསྒོམ་སྒྲུབ་བྱ་བ་ཉམས་པར་འགྱུར།

One's activities of studying, reflection, and meditation practice will deteriorate.

དེ་ཕྱིར་འཛའ་ཤེས་ཁྱིམ་དང་སྦྱིན་བདག་ཁྱིམ།

Therefore, in the householder's home or a benefactor's home,

ཀུན་ལ་ཆགས་ཞེན་ཡིད་ལ་མི་བྱེད་སྤོངས།

Abandon all attachment and non-contemplation.

There is a karmic quality and karmic energy of being attached to material things. But it is all just a momentary reflection, a dream quality. By becoming too attached to the material world, we forego the practice of meditation and study.

Even if we are uncomfortable, by abandoning attachment, we can mentally make ourselves comfortable. For example, if we must sleep on the hard ground, at least we can be grateful that it is not wet and muddy. With this mental gratitude, the situation becomes more comfortable. Our comfort is how we conceptualize things in our mind as being okay or not okay. We must understand how to detach within certain limits—to make ourselves satisfied with the conditions that are available and with what is practical. If we are too dependent on material things and do not know how to detach from comfort and luxury, then we will not be able to find a way to survive. We should be happy with whatever we have.

The teaching is trying to make us more flexible and capable of practice in any circumstance. Be happy with whatever you have; that is the best way to think about it.

37. Avoiding Harsh Speech

བཞི་པ་ཚིག་རྩུབ་སྤང་བ་སྤྱང་པ་ནི།
Fourth, avoiding harsh speech:

རྩུབ་མོའི་ཚིག་གིས་གཞན་གྱི་སེམས་གསོད་ན།
If one destroys the mind of another with harsh words,

བྱང་ཆུབ་སེམས་དཔའི་སྤྱོད་པ་ཉམས་གྱུར་པས།
The conduct of one's warm-hearted mind will decrease.

དེ་ཕྱིར་གཞན་གྱི་སེམས་ནི་གསོད་མི་རུང་།
Therefore, it is improper to destroy the minds of others;

རྩུབ་མོ་ཚིག་ནི་རྒྱུན་དུ་སྤང་བར་བྱ།
Constantly avoid rough words.

We must be careful to avoid using harsh speech, as it is a non-virtuous action that may easily wound the heart or feelings of others. By avoiding such language at any cost, we exhibit behavior that is characteristic of the enlightened mind. We should remember to always be mindful of our speech. Before we speak, we should know what we are saying, who we are speaking to, and how we are speaking.

Mindfulness of speech is a meditation in itself. It gives us stability and clarity in our speech. People who lack this concept will always be harsh in their language and will never change. As practitioners, we must pay attention to our language.

38. Ways to Renounce Ignorance

གསུམ་པ་ཉོན་མོངས་སྤང་ཚུལ་བསླབ་པ་ནི།

Third [of the five points of advice], training in the way to abandon afflictions:

ཉོན་མོངས་དུག་ལྔ་གཡོས་ནས་གཉེན་པོ་ཡིས།

When the five poisons or afflictions arise, it is difficult to repel them with antidotes.

བློག་དགའ་གཉེན་པོ་རང་ཤར་རང་གྲོལ་གྱིས།

Apply a practice of self-arising and self-liberation.

རིག་པའི་མཚོན་བཟུང་ཉོན་མོངས་དུག་ལྔ་གང་།

Grasp the weapon of Rigpa and [focus directly] on the five emotional poisons.

དང་པོ་སྐྱེས་མ་ཐག་ཏུ་འབྱུར་འཛོམས་བྱེད།

First, immediately as they are born, cut through [these] thoughts as they come to mind.

This stanza gives us two ways to renounce ignorance.

One is according to Dho, by applying an antidote when the five poisons arise. The antidote of anger is loving kindness. The antidote to attachment is generosity. The antidote of jealously is flexibility, openness, and spaciousness. The antidote of pride is calmness, simplicity, and humility. The antidote of ignorance is clear understanding and being free from doubt.

If one is a practitioner of Dzogchen, then leave everything as it is. In plain language, just leave it alone. It will be okay. In a more technical term, we call this self-liberation. In Dzogchen, we say "leave as it is, and it will liberate by itself."

So, we need to either think about these poisons and apply an antidote to overcome them, or practice Dzogchen and let the poisons liberate by themselves the moment they take place. According to Dzogchen, using the weapon of awareness, we can focus directly on the poisons, and they will liberate. Then, just let it be and rest in the natural state of mind.

ACTUAL PRACTICE

39. Advice for Serving Others

བཞི་པ་གཞན་དོན་བསྒྲུབ་པ་ལ་བསླབ་པ་ནི།

Fourth [of the five points of advice], advice for achieving benefit for others:

དྲན་ཤེས་ལྡན་པ་སྨྲ་ཤེས་དོན་གོ་བ།

Have mindful awareness, understand meanings and speak clearly.

མི་ལུས་གཅང་མ་ཐོབ་པའི་གནས་སྐབས་འདི།

In this state of having a pure human body,

རང་བས་གཞན་གྱི་དོན་ནི་གཙོ་ཆེ་བས།

It is most important to rejoice in others' welfare.

ཡེངས་མེད་རྩེ་གཅིག་གཞན་དོན་སྒྲུབ་པར་བྱེད།

Undistractedly and single-pointedly, accomplish benefit for others.

While we have achieved the level of a human being with a human body, if we are not able to make our lives more meaningful, purposeful, and beneficial for other sentient beings, then we are not fulfilling what we are meant to while in this form. We are not achieving what we could be achieving.

We mustn't focus only on ourselves. Sometimes, focusing on ourselves is needed, but not all the time. The text is saying that we should focus on the benefit of all sentient beings by learning to be of service to others.

40. Dedication of Practice

ཕྱི་མ་དགེ་བ་རྫོགས་བྱང་དུ་བསྔོ་བ་ནི།
Fifth [of the five points of advice], dedicating virtue for complete enlightenment:

དུས་གསུམ་དགེ་བ་སྒྲུབ་པ་མ་ལུས་ཀུན།
All of one's virtuous deeds of the three times (past, present, and future), without exception,

ཁམས་གསུམ་འགྲོ་ཀུན་སྡུག་བསྔལ་བསལ་བའི་ཕྱིར།
Dispel the suffering of all beings in the Three Realms (Desire, Form, and Formless).

འཁོར་གསུམ་རྣམ་དག་དག་པའི་ཤེས་རབ་ཀྱིས།
With the wisdom of the genuine purity of the three spheres (agent, action, and object),

སྐུ་གསུམ་དབྱེར་མེད་བྱང་ཆུབ་འཐོབ་ཕྱིར་བསྔོ།།
I dedicate so that I may attain the indivisible Three Bodies of Enlightenment (Bön Ku (Primordial Body), Dzog Ku (Perfection Body) and Trul Ku (Manifestation Body)).

Simply put, dedication means giving something—allowing it to be of benefit for others.

The dedication of our practice, and any merit generated by it, is for the benefit of all beings in the past, present, and future. By dedicating the merit, we are rescuing it. Otherwise, the text says the value of our practice can be insecure. Without dedication, even eons of practice could be destroyed or damaged in a moment of anger or ignorance—or by any of the five poisons. Dedication safely locks away the merit with oneself and all beings so that it cannot be damaged.

Often, we grasp onto these as objective things—the merits that were dedicated and oneself as the dedicator. So, these three principals of the dedicator, the dedication, and to whom we dedicate need to be realized within the state of emptiness. And within that emptiness, if we can dedicate, that is known as the great threefold seizing (*Khor Sum Mig Med*). You are seizing that merit—or sealing it so it never is wasted. That is the importance of dedication.

V

Conclusion

41. Genuine Practice

གསུམ་པ་མཇུག་གི་དོན་བསྡུ་བ་ལ་གསུམ་ལས། ༈
This Conclusion has three parts:

དང་པོ་ལག་ལེན་འཁྱལ་མེད་བསྟན་པ་ནི།
First, an explanation of authentic practice:

བློ་གྲོས་དམན་ཞིང་སྦྱང་བ་ཆུང་བ་ཡིས།
With limited intelligence and little experience of wisdom,

མཁས་པ་དགྱེས་པའི་སྙེབ་སྦྱོར་མ་ཤེས་ཀྱང་།
Even [though I may not] know the poetics to delight the Wise Ones,

རྒྱལ་བའི་བཀའ་དང་འཕགས་པའི་ལུང་དང་གཉིས།
Both the words of the Victor, and the transmissions of Wise Ones,

རང་སེམས་ཤར་དང་གསུམ་པོ་འཁྱལ་མེད་བསྟན།
As well as my own experiences, have all been genuinely illustrated.

Humbly, the master who wrote this, His Holiness, Kündun Sonam Lodrö, who was the 21st sMenri Trizin, is saying that he himself may not be a great practitioner, that he is not such a great master, and that he does not have great intellect or wisdom, but rather, genuinely, based on the teachings of the Enlightened Ones (Sangye) and the great masters, but especially on his own

CONCLUSION

experience, he has come to the realizations he has written in this text.

These verses are practical guidelines about how we should apply our practice in the circumstances as he has mentioned in the stanzas above. These circumstances he describes are not just those of his life but are genuinely applicable to everyone. He says this is all truly illustrated by his own experiences and on the basis of the Sangye and higher masters. This shows his humility.

He doesn't say, "This is my way, I have the transmission, so follow me." He simply says, "I am ordinary. I'm just a practitioner." He says, "I know I am not able to go to the depths of Sangye Tönpa Shenrab's teaching."

This teacher was a manifestation of the wisdom deity. He was originally known as an emanation of wisdom deity "Mawe Senge Namtrul." Although the author of this book is the manifestation aspect of the wisdom deity, he shows that no matter how wise and high we are, we should not be proud but instead be simple. This is the nature of authentic practice.

42. Acknowledgement

གཉིས་པ་དམ་པ་རྣམས་ལ་བཟོད་པར་གསོལ་བ་ནི།

Second, requesting patience from the Holy Ones:

སངས་རྒྱས་དགོངས་པ་མཐའ་དང་བྲལ་བ་ལ།

The quality of an enlightened mind is boundaryless.

བདག་འདྲ་བློ་དམན་གཏིང་དཔག་དཀའ་བ་ཡིས།

For those of lesser intelligence like me, it is difficult to understand its depth.

ནོར་འཁྲུལ་ཉེས་འགལ་ཅི་མཆིས་སྐྱབས་ཡུལ་དང་།

Whatever mistakes, faults, or contradictions herein, to the Enlightened Ones and

མཁས་གྲུབ་རྣམས་ལ་བཟོད་པར་མཛོད་པར་ཞུ།

To the scholar-saints, I ask for your patience.

Here, His Holiness, Sherab Gongyal, states he is not capable of fully understanding the true nature of the Sangye's mind or the Enlightened Ones. He is not able to understand the true depth of their knowledge.

He says that, because of this fact, if he has made any mistakes in this teaching, he apologizes to the Enlightened Ones for those mistakes. The vastness of the Sangye's mind of enlightenment is not something he can judge and understand completely. Therefore, he apologizes for any mistakes. Again, this stanza is showing his genuine humility.

CONCLUSION

43. Dedication and Aspirational Prayer

གསུམ་པ་འདི་བཅམས་པའི་བསྔོ་བ་དང་མཛད་བྱང་ནི།

Third, the dedication and the colophon of this composition:

འདི་བྱུང་དགེ་བའི་རྩ་བས་འགྲོ་བ་ཀུན།

Whatever roots of virtue [arise from this composition], to all beings

ཀུན་རྫོབ་དོན་དམ་བྱང་ཆུབ་སེམས་མཆོག་བསྔོ།

I dedicate both the relative and absolute supreme mind of enlightenment,

སྲིད་དང་ཞི་བའི་མཐའ་ལ་མི་གནས་པར།

Without falling into either side of cyclic existence or enlightenment.

ཤེས་རབ་སྨྲ་སེང་ཉིད་དང་མཚུངས་པར་ཤོག

May all become as the Wisdom Deity (Sherab Mawé Sengé).

ཅེས་པ་གནམ་བོན་རྒྱ་གར་དཔོན་པོ་༸སྨན་རིའི་སྐྱ་མདུན་ཤེས་རབ་དགོངས་རྒྱལ་གྱིས་སྦྱར་བ་བདེ་ལེགས་སུ་གྱུར་ཅིག་དགོའོ་ཞེས་སོ།།

This was composed by Nam Bön Gyakar Wonpo, HH the 21st sMenri Küdun Sherab Gongyal. May it be virtuous!

Here, His Holiness dedicates whatever merit and quality he receives from composing this book to all sentient beings, so that they may benefit from his merit. He prays and wishes that each and every being who is practicing and who was connecting with this teaching, may achieve the enlightened body of the wisdom deity, Mawé Sengé. That is his prayer and his dedication.

This dedication concludes the teaching of the Forty-Three Guiding Principles for an Enlightened Mind.

www.ingramcontent.com/pod-product-compliance
Lightning Source LLC
Chambersburg PA
CBHW060525080526
44586CB00012B/614